AF473664

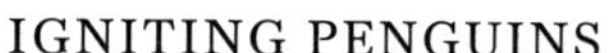

IGNITING PENGUINS

Rachel Lumsden

Igniting Penguins

A Manifesto for Painting

SCHEIDEGGER & SPIESS

Copy-editing Louise Stein
Proofreading Simon Cowper
Design Katrina Wiedner, onwhite.studio
Printing and binding gugler* Drucksinn, Melk/Donau
Set in Parallel I–IV, designed by Joana Siniavskaja

Verlag Scheidegger & Spiess
Niederdorfstrasse 54
8001 Zurich
Switzerland
www.scheidegger-spiess.ch

Scheidegger & Spiess is supported by the Federal Office of Culture with a general subsidy for the years 2021–2024.

ISBN 978-3-03942-146-6

The book is published parallel to the exhibition *Rachel Lumsden – The Blazing Hot Moment und andere Funkensprünge*, which is showing at the Kunstmuseum Thurgau, Kartause Ittingen, from 2 July to 17 December 2023.

Also available in German translation under the title *Ritt auf der Wildsau – Manifest für die Malerei* (ISBN 978-3-03942-145-9).

For Norman, Nellie, Vera, Neil and Grace.
Still here in my heart.

Table of Contents

Foreword

Forewords should be treated in the same way as photographs of paintings: you study them briefly and then turn to the real thing.

This is a book on the subject of figurative painting, its status on the contemporary art scene and the experience of being a figurative painter. It's written from an unashamedly idiosyncratic perspective, in eleven chapters with a prologue about a girl born in northern England half a century ago.

Most important for me is the painterly process and the question: What actually happens when the tip of a brush – or a floor mop – touches the canvas?

There are three reasons for writing this little book. The first and main trigger was the handwritten reply from a Swiss art museum director, to whom I had presented a catalogue of work with an invitation to visit me in the studio. He politely declined, declaring that he missed the *rote Faden* – the "red thread" of continuity in my work. Although I was disappointed by his answer and suspected that the missing thread had sprung from a bias rooted in gender aesthetics, I let his misinterpretation stand. I thought to myself that the paths of male and female artists do not follow the same course – and archived his postcards. This was the beginning of an interesting collection of prejudices, erroneous views and statements about painting that I have come across in the Swiss art world, a collection that is now ripe for closer analysis.

The second reason is that such a book would have been very useful to me when I first moved from Britain to Switzerland at the beginning of the new millennium. The Swiss art scene and its environment have their own peculiarities when it comes to dealing with figurative painting, especially *painterly figuration*, where motif emerges out of the blobs and smears of the sticky material substance known as oil paint. I often felt like the proverbial ox in a ditch – which might have enjoyed a bit of light reading matter before trying to scramble out.

The third trigger was the huge but strangely empty thought bubble that formed with Covid, in the spring of 2020. The task was to sit in this bubble and do something with it.

Sometimes, while writing, I had a reader in mind whom I call the *Little Painter*, who appears from time to time in this text and who probably relates all too well to my situation as a figurative painter in my first years abroad.

But like painting, this writing is also a bit of a shape-shifter and has changed its form during the writing process: At the beginning I called it a manifesto, but it is also a treatise, a story, a field report, a survival guide ... and probably a lot more. That's fine; I've pretty much let the book take its own course and be what it wants to be. Except to be boring.

For those still missing the red thread of continuity, a little hint: it's about *painting*.

Rachel Lumsden, January 2023

Prologue

Light doing overtime – A slide carousel

Click.

A long time ago, at least before I was born, a dragon died on the flat roof of our garage leaving nothing but its bones. Dad would put me up on his shoulders so I could get my chin over the lip of the roof to look sideways to where the heavy bones and flat iron skull lay. An iron skull is better suited to fire-breathers and the flatter it is, the better it can fly.

Click.

The assumption that dragons with flat iron heads could fly better was proven correct on a trip to the newly built terminal at Newcastle Airport. We sat on posh leather sofas in the panorama lounge, tea and scones on the low coffee table, watching the planes fly in and out: long slender tubes, with flat iron skulls and knives for wings – copied from dragons, it was obvious.

The carpet was tangerine with vacuum tracks; you could tell it was new. Chunky concrete columns sprouted from it to hold up the ceiling. And the furniture was almost as elegant as the furniture that Dad built for us in the garage in Throckley called *Danish Modern style*.

Click.

Newcastle-upon-Tyne, pungent with the soapy hops smell of Newcastle Brown Ale, was more a city of ships than planes, however, with shipyards at Wallsend near Tynemouth and more supertankers looming over the brick terraces of Gateshead.

So the fact that you had the remains of a dead dragon on the garage roof was special, but no more so than the colossal ship bodies dwarfing the neighbourhoods, and when they were launched, it seemed like a whole landmass was sliding out to sea and away.

Click.

Death in Throckley lived in the old quarry, at the bottom of the road, cordoned off by a high wire fence and undergrowth. The quarry floor was cracked and crusted like a parched desert and was, in fact, quicksand.

We watched as Mister Hedley's gardener, ladder under arm, climbed down to the bottom to retrieve a couple of runaway chickens. The chickens, too light really to sink into the quicksand, were nevertheless stuck. The gardener laid the ladder over the treacherous terrain, crawled over it rung by rung, clamped the poultry to his chest and made it back to safe ground. Padlocking the gate behind him and throwing the chickens back over the wall into the garden he turned on us.

We had watched *Operation Chicken Rescue,* noses pressed to the chain-link fence, excited at the possibility of chickens – and gardener – being swallowed by quicksand.

"Divvent gan doon there yew lot!" he shouted at us grimly.

"Wey?"

"Coz ye'll dii ye doylem!"

Click.

You had to go and see Uncle Alf for an encounter with living deadeye black. His skin was pink and black, especially on his back. Each little micro-skin-pore was tattooed with minerally coal dust from the mines, which he could never get off, even after Auntie Laura had been at him with the loofah. Our knowledge of quicksand and its exciting dangers also came from their household. They had a bigger TV set than we did and on the weekend there was the Saturday matinee, or "the fillum", usually a western or musical or some hybrid of the two. We gawked like idiots at Comanches in ambush and cacti and belts full of bullets and gun-slinging baddies sinking in quicksand until all you could see was the black cowboy hat. My sister Helen, trying to grasp the plot, kept asking "What's he doing? What's happening now?" and nearly drove me up the wall.

In my eyes her questions were pointless because the television as a thing in life was completely untrustworthy – I had already gathered that at infant school. We finished school at half past three in the afternoon, and by the time we got home in winter, it was already pitch dark, such raven blackness around the house that it seemed impossible for it still to be light elsewhere. And yet as soon as you switched on the TV to watch the children's programme "Play School", there was plain daylight, properly boxed in glass and wood. Such a lie.

Click.

At the top of the street and across the adjoining Hexham Road resided the green, behind a long, high slope of brick-buttressed wall with dripping pipes at intervals, staining the red brick with dark, vertical streaks. The glinting wet moss was already a clue to the colour on the other side of the wall in the now-disused and drained Victorian reservoir: a thick and slimy green, spectacularly staining white knee socks when you waded through it. It worked best on my little sister in the pale-blue pushchair. Stank too. That was the real, damp green.

For the other green it was best to sneak over to the bins at the Working Men's Club up by the bus shelter, quietly lift off the metal lids there at the back of the car park, and rummage through the rubbish. The colour of the treasure to be unearthed here was the dry green of discarded bingo-booklets, which had a whole rainbow of colours inside at the tear-off fold. These lay like jewels among the cigarette butts and crumpled packets of pork scratchings in the pongy metal drum.

I collected them in quantities, tied them up in small blocks with rubber bands, and hid them in the toy cupboard. They were smelly though and Mammy had a good nose, so my colour swatches were gone again as regularly as I brought the dry green home.

Click.

The lower shelf of the library bus, next to tiny stools with screw-on legs, went "far beyond the jungles and the burning deserts to the bright blue ocean that stretched in all directions".[1] Within a drab linen-bound cover, on wafer thin pages of double-sided saturation, yellow to blue, blue to pink, pink to grey, floated the *black tiger* and the *yellow creature* and I was their castaway.

Click.

The colour of bruise wasn't just to be found on arms and legs after an afternoon swinging from the motorbike tree in the little copse but was also to be found out on the moors behind Hadrian's Wall, where the wind stirred the tussocks of ochre grasses, into the carmine and violet of heather and the amber of curling bracken leaves. We'd roam all day through this seep of colour, between earth and sky, wading too in the little river, pulling out handfuls of fossilised twigs. At day's end when darkness blanketed the car windows, the smell of bruised moorland accompanied us to the back seat of the Renault and came home with us in our hair, in every fibre of our clothes.

Click.

The stillness in Throckley lived in the very last house on the street and had a black tongue. Where the garden ended, the fields and woods began.

When you entered the house, you left the normal world of sound behind and stepped into a dome of concentrated silence. Although it was not really quiet in the house: one could hear the light jingling of chains as the two birds hopped to and fro from one side of the perch to another. The white crested cockatoo didn't like the ankle chain and put its head feathers up when you tried to touch it before pecking at your hand. The African red-bellied parrot glared at you with a round yellow eye, a tiny black iris stranded in the centre.

The ground floor was open throughout, from the glazed entrance and conservatory at the front to the glass doors and garden at the back. In spite of windows on both sides it always seemed dim in there. But as the two birds lived in the winter garden on street-side, one never had to venture deep into that room. Where the boy was. And the machine. I never knew the name of the boy in the machine, backlit by the garden window, but sometimes he'd wake up and turn his head towards me, neck disappearing into the pleated collar which bulged, sagged and bulged again, in time with the bellows inside the metal cylinder that enclosed his body.

The birds tripped back and forth on their perches, sometimes opening their beaks, their tongues black and muscular, like the graphite leads in Dad's propelling pencils.

Click.

In summer the light in Throckley worked overtime. Long after sundown there was a sky-brightness over roofs and trees and the gardens below, the bright brick facades of the houses, the cars on the curbside; even the pavement exuded a kind of afterglow.

Before bedtime I walked barefoot on the narrow strip of grass in the front garden, cup of cocoa cradled in my hands. My blue nightdress had a pink-and-white embroidered bodice. The blue was deep indigo, so deep it bordered on the nocturnal. I was completely in tune with it; the indigo was me and I was the indigo.

Each blade of grass on the glowing lawn had a barely perceptible edge of silver where the lawnmower had clipped it and the criss-cross glint of silver made the green even richer, more real and solid than the light-blue Ford Cortina that Alan's older brother was washing on the driveway nearby, humming along with the car radio.

In the bedroom upstairs, the curtains were already drawn across the half-open window. I lay on my back in bed, watching the overtime light effortlessly penetrate the loose warp and weft of the fabric, the hemmed edges like white spray. I could still hear the car radio playing: "This year I'm off to sunny Spain, Y viva España".

Although the heaviness of sleep came to claim my body, my mind remained awake and light, flowing around the colours, scents and sounds of the evening that were now within me.

I remember that. I remember the six-year-old, her cup of cocoa, her indigo being. I not only remember her. She's still here with me. Especially when I am painting. Maybe because she was already the painter I later became. Or the physicist and land artist I didn't become. The furniture maker I am as a hobbyist. The drunk I managed to avoid becoming. The bird lover I cherish being. But above all, I encounter her when I paint.

Painting is my gate into the life of the senses. My possibility, as an adult, to connect again and again with worlds, with the past, with the present and with the not yet or never formed.

That's what we share, she as a child and me as a painter: the ecstasy of being connected.

1 From the illustrated childrens' book *Captain Slaughterboard Drops Anchor* by Mervyn Peake, London: Eyre & Spottiswoode, 1945.

1

Can I paint a tree with birds?

So, can I paint a tree with birds?

Doh – course you can paint a tree with birds.

Then, can I paint a tree with birds so that it becomes a beautiful, simple and joyful painting to behold, a picture without irony, pessimistic refraction, symbolism, or art quote?

Go ahead, if that's what floats your boat ...

Moreover, am I allowed not only to paint such a picture but also to exhibit it?

Err, well, I suppose ... let me get back to you on that ... Hmm. What would it mean for your hard-won reputation as a contemporary artist? Maybe don't try it out here. Not just yet, because painting still isn't quite the thing here, even in 2021 – especially when it's trying to represent something. And trees, birds, beauty? Really? (You big girl's blouse!) Better to leave all that to nature, eh?

A long time ago, in 2001 my sister-in-law and her partner visited us in the eastern Swiss city of St. Gallen. We'd never met before. It turned out that the girlfriend was a video artist and worked with one of the biggest Swiss art stars. She asked me what I did. No sooner had the word "painter" crossed my lips, incredulity, even disdain spread across her face as though no self-respecting woman with a modicum of intelligence could possibly engage with such a backward medium. Sure enough, a clipped verbal rebuke followed in which it was made clear to me that in Switzerland painting – especially figurative painting – wasn't considered to be a contemporary artistic medium at all.

It was quite literally a conversation killer, occurring most unfortunately at the beginning of the visit, and the awkwardness of the exchange hovered over the little Biedermeier table where we drank strong coffee from plain bone-china cups and ate a custardy "bee-sting" cake until the Swiss art superstar herself arrived, as vivacious as her videos and gracious to boot, and our visitors steamed off back to Basel with her.

The whiff of cowpat

In September 2021 in the *Neue Zürcher Zeitung* (NZZ), Christoph Blocher, the right-wing alpha dog of Swiss politics, was to be found deftly parrying the critical questions of two journalists.[2] The accompanying photo showed this wily old croc in front of his painting collection, with Albert Anker's nostalgic *home and hearth* paintings of rural idylls from the 19th century particularly prominent.

I realised that this photo offered an apt visual metaphor for the fate of figurative painting: right-wing conservative nationalism had taken it into protective custody; it is a victim of the culture war over modernism.

How could this have happened?

Perhaps because Switzerland was spared the existential shock of the First World War, the break with the past that caused many European countries to radically turn away from the aesthetics that had prevailed until then.

Its prosperity, its central location, the four national languages and, above all, its political neutrality had made

Switzerland in those years a centre of attraction for artists and intellectuals who wanted to escape the turmoil of war in their countries of origin.

In 1916, far away from the barrage of the fronts, a dazzlingly bright, if short-lived, flare rose into the sky from Zurich's old town: in the Cabaret Voltaire, Dadaism declared war on the prevailing status quo and proclaimed itself not only anti-art, but anti-everything of bourgeois-capitalist value, which in their view was responsible for Europe's wartime misery. In the process, representational art and figurative painting in particular came into the Dadaist crosshairs. While this anarchist pulse of the avant-garde spread to Paris, Weimar, Dessau and Berlin after the end of the war, it died out in Switzerland.

In 1918, when workers' revolutions crushed empires in Germany and Austria, in Switzerland the military subdued the general strike under threat of armed force. After that, the Helvetic focus turned to evoking national unity and a conservative Switzerland in the spirit of the founding fathers. In the cultural sphere, the focus returned to traditional genres of art, including figurative painting.

The handful of Swiss artists committed to the avant-garde moved to Paris or to the Bauhaus in Weimar and Dessau, where they were considered to be "particularly progressive", while in Switzerland the forces of inertia remained strong.[3]

If modernism was to succeed in taking shape and making space for itself in this environment, it not only had to throw all traditions, conventions and obligations overboard with aesthetic rigour, but it also had to establish for itself a rigid habitus. This habitus is still present in the art world today as a purist aesthetic: intellect ranks high above the sensory; purity of colour and geometric forms are considered far superior to the limitations of the representational – think here of Johannes Itten or Max Bill, for example.

Is it surprising then that figurative painting as a serious art genre in Switzerland seems to have ended with Hodler? After that, it was tolerated at best in the context of "Neue Sachlichkeit" (New Objectivity) or the Basler

Rot-Blau movement (1920s–1930s). Even the exhibition *Zeitprobleme in der Schweizer Malerei und Plastik* (Problems of Time in Swiss Painting and Sculpture) curated by Wilhelm Wartmann and Siegfried Giedion in 1936 at the Kunsthaus Zürich, in which figurative – albeit mainly Surrealist – and abstract works demonstrated an unproblematic coexistence, did nothing to change this. As New Objectivity waned, the anti-sensorial, rational thinking of the Avant Garde finally claimed the leading role.

Apart from loners like Willy Guggenheim alias Varlin, who continued to paint figuratively, the great debates in painting were fought out between representatives of concrete abstraction/constructivism and the adherents of non-concrete abstraction. The art-going public, of course always out of step with the artistic elite wherever in the world, continued to revere figuration to the extent that the 1955 Paul Klee exhibition in Kunstmuseum St. Gallen caused a huge scandal, with Klee's semi abstract, schematic, musical-notation-like works being perceived to be no better than infantile scribbles.[4]

While the Swiss art public was still struggling to come to terms with the beginnings of abstraction, Abstract Expressionism was already on the wane in the USA and was being squeezed by Pop Art, although in the late forties and well into the fifties it had even been covertly promoted by the CIA as part of the "Congress for Cultural Freedom" programme as a counter-movement to Socialist Realism in Communism.[5]

By the 1960s, figurative painting in der Schweiz was already considered so conservative and traditional by the Swiss art establishment that it almost completely disappeared from practice, teaching and criticism. The death knell came within the context of the seminal exhibition *When Attitudes Become Form* curated by Harald Szeemann in 1969 in Bern, just as American painter, Philip Guston, one of the pioneers of Abstract Expressionism in the USA, was returning to figuration.

In the seventies, figurative painting in Switzerland was leashed between the hearthside and the cattle trough and no longer had a chance of being taken seriously as a contemporary medium or legitimate form of expression. Actually, worse still, looking at how museums represent Modernism in *la Suisse*, especially in their online collections where theoretically they would have endless space to show different interests, it looks as though figurative painting outside of Surrealism didn't even really make it into Modernism.

By contrast, in Germany, Baselitz, Richter, Kiefer et al. became important positions of international standing. The same is true for Great Britain: the figurative painting of the School of London, a group initiated by R. B. Kitaj with Lucian Freud, Francis Bacon, Leon Kossoff, Frank Auerbach, Michael Andrews and David Hockney, similarly left its mark throughout the 20th century. So did the London Group with painters like Walter Sickert and Paula Rego.

Occasionally, from time to time an angry little figurative painting-pimple flares up on the otherwise smooth skin of the Swiss art scene – as it did in the eighties, for example, with Martin Disler's or Dieter Roth's night-long painting binges – to explode hot and sticky onto the art scene. But Clearasil is always to hand, and all the while the ghost of Johannes Itten, dressed as in life as priest-cum-monkish schoolmaster, watches vigilantly over all.

It should come as no surprise that nowadays many Swiss painters are still to be found in the camp of geometric, hard-edged (concrete) abstraction and colour field painting. Sometimes representational painting makes a guest appearance as one of the arrows in an artist's quiver. Then painting is pursued as a kind of sideline, parallel to other means of expression, and so always remains subordinate to an overall artistic strategy. Artists who paint intermittently like this rarely describe themselves as "painters" (in fact they nearly fall over themselves in their hurry to make it clear that they are *not* painters – what a god-forsaken backwater that would be) but rather the more innocuous "visual arts practitioner".

When figuration is actually practised in earnest, it often comes across as cool, conceptual and flat as if it had not only been squeezed out of a camera lens but has also had to be constantly and suspiciously monitored under the creed of "thou shalt not" because, after all, the traps of beauty and painterly figuration lurk everywhere.

And what shalt thou not?

Thou shalt not covet thy neighbour's eye, nor tempt it to pleasure. In particular, shalt thou disdain and repulse *Geste* (the gestural) for it has the reputation of being – oops – a vehicle for emotionality. Or for sentimentalism – so sayeth the Art-Lord. Yet the "gestural", or rather its traces, are only testimonies to expedience, to the practicality of paint application, and to velocity. Mark-making and tracks in the paint are simply characteristics of the painting process rather than an assault on the emotional life of the viewer.

Fortunately, painting, which has often been pronounced dead, always rises again. For at least ten years, it has been pushing through the hard ground of Swiss art schools in all its wondrous facets. A whole generation of young painters has rediscovered the unoccupied niche of figurative painting for themselves, a niche that they can fill with little competition from the older generation, who more or less abandoned it wholesale – it hardly even requires gate-crashing.[6] As students at art school they want to learn it and would prefer to be aided and abetted in their endeavours rather than being admonished and told to get their fingers away from the fire.

But perhaps it's better not to underestimate the sheer daunting task of teaching something that older generations of artist-teachers haven't got a handle on themselves, because not only was the skillset abandoned and never handed on, but the ability to see and relate, to understand, to talk about and evaluate it also disappeared with it. There's nothing like a figurative painting to cause confusion and suspicion – because how do you judge the flippin' thing?

Malerisch versus painterly

Words are important too.

I learned German at night school and *on the job* – as a painting teacher in art schools.

It gradually dawned on me, for instance, that the German adjective *malerisch* is not the same at all as the word "painterly" in English but is far nearer in essence to the English word "quaint", or "picturesque". "Painterly", on the other hand, is used almost exclusively to characterise the qualities of a painting – i.e. being made and expressed with and through the substance of paint, within the parameters of what paint as a material can most readily do.

The fact that *malerisch* can pose as an apparent equivalent for "painterly", although it carries a completely different meaning, presents contemporary figurative painting with a dilemma: the language used to conceptualise art and its processes creates confusion – and smears a sticky syrup all over it.

But hang on a minute – wasn't the word "painterly" originally derived directly from the German word *malerisch*? Wasn't it Ernst Gombrich who took the word from the Swiss art historian Heinrich Wölfflin? Wölfflin used "painterly" to refer to an array of visual qualities occurring in painting, like broad brushstrokes, the breaking up of contours through contrasting colours, broken tones and chromatic progression. So *malerisch* was once part of a robust vocabulary that art commentators used to discuss painting, *what* it does and *how* it does it.

What happened? When did it get so soft as to be allowed to lean towards the meaning "quaint" and "picturesque" and is it me or is there a whiff of cowpat in the room?

Anti-painting painting

If you are a young would-be artist attending a foundation course or an undergraduate degree there are one or two accepted courses for using paint as a figurative medium that won't immediately get you into trouble with your tutors and later with the curators – and one of them is the anti-painting position.

Anti-painting relies on wit, breaking with conventions and freshness. It deliberately pretends to be unskilled by negating the technical craft side that "painterly" painting always has. It's snotty, cheeky, impetuous, uncomplicated – in other words, rather cool and likeable, resembling street art on canvas. It is widespread among the older generation of Swiss artists because in the sixties and seventies they mostly received training as graphic artists, either in the form of a four-year vocational apprenticeship or in a graphics class. At that time, there was no other form of art training in Switzerland so anyone who wanted to study fine art had to apply to the academies in Germany, Austria, Italy, or France.

So those who stayed knew not only how to design fonts, lay out a book, or choose a printing grid, they used paint too – but often more as a linear drawing medium rather than applying it in squelchy masses of overlaid colour or dragging one fatty blob through another. That kind of painting, its history and its practice, simply wasn't part of the curriculum. The approach to painting was therefore autodidactic, not school-based and ahistorical, even if they were visual professionals at a very high level. This is precisely what gives the anti-painting painting camp a lot of freshness and charm.

It goes without saying that they could not then become the standard bearers of *Grande peinture*, of layered, track-strewn *painterly figuration*, as practised in Britain or Germany, for example. The anti-painting position became a refusal and rejection of painting itself.

Therefore a painting that had layers was considered by the anti-painters to be irrecoverably lost, while one with a few flatly applied shapes and sketchy contours seemed almost finished. As a general rule of thumb, if more than two thirds of the gesso primer on the canvas was covered, the painting had already failed. What's more, the random pattern of paint blobs and streaks on the studio floor was always more interesting than anything deliberately placed on the canvas. This creed still prevails today.

Painting as installation

The second way our art student can get away with figurative painting is to turn it into installation.

Whether you remove the splattered ground sheets from the floor of your studio or the paintings from the wall, the art establishment will take it better if you display the works on A-frames like advertising billboards or hang them from a zip wire. For installation is a recognised *modus operandi,* even installations with figurative painting. Exhibiting painting as an installation is by no means just a strategy of artists who want to make it inside art institutions with their paintings. Art institutions also participate in this arrangement, as it allows them to open their doors to painting.

I am suddenly reminded of the somewhat hesitant probing of a curator who asked whether I could imagine painting the large panorama window in the side-lit hall of her institution. This installation painting would have accompanied a large thematic exhibition, for which she considered my classical paintings on panels to be ... unsuitable. Hmm. Finger-paint on the windows instead? *That's* what you really want from me?

These thoughts run through my mind as I make my way between overlapping sheets of stained canvas, dangling loosely on wires from the glass ceiling of another museum. I'm struck by how this arrangement diverts my attention from the single work and scatters it throughout the space, as if the artist and museum's intention had been to create a forest – or possibly a yard goods emporium, to be viewed as a whole, where dialogue with a single work is not possible. This, of course, makes it difficult to fall under the spell of a single painting and its idiosyncrasies.

In 1942, the Picture of the Month exhibitions at the National Gallery in London were the opposite of painting as installation where the individual work becomes invisible. At the beginning of the war, the museum's contents had been moved to the Manod slate mines in Wales for safekeeping. When the German bombing raids became less frequent, it was considered acceptable for a single painting at a time to be shown in the National Gallery – the Picture of the Month brought to London from Snowdonia. News of the arrival of a new painting spread like wildfire through the city, bringing hundreds of visitors to the museum every day, all drawn by the spell of this one, single painting. Although the circumstances of this time were different, the idea of a single painting in an otherwise empty museum still touches me today. The Picture of the Month programme is still going on, by the way, and is imitated around the globe.

What makes an artist?

Art education sets out to develop students' critical thinking and artistic practice. For instance: When you use an easel it means you are adopting a framework that has been created much earlier, which almost automatically leads to a particular outcome or end product.

Art education encourages you to reflect on where and why this framework came into being, whether it is still appropriate, or whether you have allowed complacency to choose for you. So it can happen that you start your studies as a painter and finish as a filmmaker – or vice versa.

Studying art does not mean that every art student will become an artist. Conversely, there are recognised artists with important work who have never seen the inside of an art school – think of Francis Bacon, for example. So what makes you an artist if it's not your education?

Perhaps it is the thorny pilgrimage that the artist makes between and after art training which is at odds with many other life choices often taken for granted in other professions – financial security, respectability, parenting, pensions, mortgages, etc., which also determine the artist. The question of parenting is an especially important consideration for female artists, who tend still to be the main carers and whose careers can easily go down the drain as a result.

Determination in the face of adverse circumstances is something of a forge through which an artist generally must pass and through which her work develops. I think of it as a kind of furnace in which artistic concerns, creative agility, broad interest, depth, commitment and self-reflection are formed. This determination is at least as important as a studio where one can experiment and develop new work year after year.

It is not necessarily the dramatic highs and lows that make up this slow and never-ending pilgrimage, although of course that can be the case. Rather, it is the small, incremental decisions that one makes and their consequences, both in one's work and in one's life, which shape this journey.

Looking back on my teenage years today, I recognise some of the crossroads that have made me who I am today – just as anyone becomes who they are through a set of circumstances and decisions.

Some were direct binary choices posed by an education system. For instance, study art. *Or* study sciences and keep painting as a recreational hobby. By then it was already clear to me that art as a hobby and a life as an artist are two completely different things.

I chose art, against the advice of guardians. Some influences were circumstantial: good teachers, bad teachers, the early death of a parent and the subsequent early departure from the family home as a minor; a brief and illuminating clash with Christian fundamentalism, an even briefer brush with radical Marxism, an opportunity at the age of seventeen to paint in a group with an artist "in residence", culminating in a group show at the contemporary art space, *The Midland Group* in Nottingham, my earliest exhibition. Around that time I had my first-ever visit to an art museum too, where in one day I saw paintings by Max Beckmann and Francis Bacon and was utterly blown away by their intense, visceral presence. I hadn't grown up in an art-aware family and until then had little idea of what art could do.

Step by step, sometimes consciously, sometimes unconsciously, I had placed my bets on the "art horse" and experienced a slow but lasting transformation ... into what? An artist? A visual arts practitioner? A perpetual student of art? A painter?

I remember back in 1997, many years after that first either-or decision, sitting outside Mulligan's Pub in Cork Street behind the Royal Academy (RA) in London drinking Guinness and chewing the fat with a fellow student, Mark, from the sculpture department. We had just attended a lecture at the RA by Marina Abramović, who at the time had a show at the Institute for Contemporary Art in London. In the light of all that we had heard and discussed earlier that evening we found it preposterous to call ourselves artists and decided to avoid such tags as much as possible. If all else failed, then he was simply a sculptor and I a painter.

No matter what label you choose for yourself, there comes a time when you realise that the decision to be an artist has stuck with you and the journey has begun. Of course, there are always ways to stop that journey, but the deeper you go and the longer you're on the road, the less likely you are to stop and quit. You don't stay in the same place for long either but are constantly busy finding the route that leads to the next artistic discovery, the passage into the new cave complex where you then work for a while. With the works that are created there, in that new, hitherto unknown place, one also lays a trail for those who want to explore something similar.

This, actually, is "the red thread of continuity" and of course involves change and development through a whole succession of choices – including which expectations one serves with one's work and whether or not these should coincide with those of the art establishment.

Whatever the reason – or the complicated interplay of reasons – for the awkward relationship with figurative painting on the Swiss contemporary scene, the question of whether it is permissible to paint and exhibit a tree full of birds in an intentionally beautiful, painterly and non-ironic way cannot really be answered by any kind of aesthetic and intellectual protectionism.

So allow me to backtrack a little and ask: Have you ever seen a crow sunbathing? The bird stock still, beak wide open, head tilted, feathers ruffled up and wings spread wide? Man, what a sight! Or has a crow ever stuck its head in your pocket and stolen your Kleenex and your house keys? So where to begin?

Perhaps like this: During Covid part 1 – the first lockdown in March 2020 – I walked across the fields in the slowly lengthening evenings and was amazed at how quickly the animals in the marshes – deer, hares, foxes, badgers – appeared where I'd never seen them before. They were neither particularly anxious nor particularly interested in this lone individual but slipped easily and naturally back into a space that noisy agriculture, a congested motorway slip road and hectic leisure and sports activities had vacated. Later at the back end of summer, as I stood between two tall dark walls of maize with bats flitting overhead, the sky still not quite drained of all light, I heard a duet between a nightingale and the electronic bleep-bleep of some farm machine reversing.

The sight and sound of animals and birds calmly pursuing their needs or interests was comforting: there was a completely different track of nature beyond the human animal who had just got out of step, a nature school offering a regular dose of reality in contrast to our anthropocentrism.

At that time, our crow Dora had injured her right foot and was convalescing in a makeshift aviary in my office. As I worked at the computer, Dora sat on a branch watching me; at times she would move in so close that I could scratch her neck with one hand as I stabbed at the keyboard with the other. To entertain her, I sometimes drew pictures of her with brush and ink on kitchen towel, to hand in case of stray poops. Dora was far less interested in her portraits than in the pleasure of pecking at the blots and dabs of sepia ink, like they might be tasty to eat, and ultimately stealing the brush from my hand (yes, she's a Dadaist).

I started collecting pictures of birds; one of them, a thrush in a rowan tree against a blue sky, was so luminous that I immediately wanted to paint it as a small format – not illustrative or realistic but painterly, so that it would become an all-round experience of cobalt blue and equally of paint and feather, bush and cadmium berry.

A studio visitor, masked and sanitised, who'd studied art in central Switzerland (years before I taught there) saw that little painting and immediately declared that I couldn't possibly exhibit *that* – but asked if he could buy it as a gift for his parents. When I asked why the bird painting could not be exhibited, the answer was simple: "Too beautiful." When I asked why he would buy it then – after he had just banished it unequivocally from the art world, he said with a sigh: "Because it is so beautiful."

Beauty, question mark

The subject of beauty (in painting) sometimes makes the art world sick to its stomach. The code goes: "Be careful not to undermine your brand with beauty or sensuality, and if you do, don't expect to be taken seriously as a contemporary artist. If you employ beauty in a work, be sure to kick it good and proper in the shins with some little twist of abjection or ironic refraction. Make it clear to the world that you know – and follow – the art code."

Since when has beauty been considered suspect? Since when does its presence throw the quality of a work into doubt, to the extent that only if it's not beautiful, must it then be good?

Here we find ourselves again at the beginning of modernism and an avant-garde that knew that the best way of jolting and challenging a complacent bourgeois society was by employing the shock of ugliness – of anti-beauty, ambivalence, provocation.

Because the natural inclination is to be attracted by beauty, its presence in a work of art is readily identified as being suspect. Is it permissible to be attracted to a contemporary work of art? Or is that already something to be reported as suspicious?

Even today, the abject and the ambivalent are the two main elements of the super-formula employed by artists to shock the "audience" out of its comfort zone.

I am typing these lines in the airport terminal at London City, now in summer 2021, and watching news clips flicker across the plasma screens in which the world is either burning or drowning. I ponder the efficiency of the CO_2 offset for the coming flight: ten little saplings = one gnarled old oak? *Really*?[7]

And at the same time I wonder why the bogus criterion of anti-beauty as the main characteristic of good art is still so zealously championed. So much so, that to paint something beautiful beautifully on a canvas must either be an act of foolishness – or of naïve provocation.

Does art not necessitate the full spectrum? Does painting not require the full frequency band from beauty to ambivalence to anti-beauty?

Subject matter matters

Fifteen years ago, an older artist colleague, B, in St. Gallen saw two of my paintings in an exhibition and felt compelled to lecture me immediately. He took me to one side for the pep talk and began by saying how much he respected my obviously stupendous painting skills and evident painterly prowess – I was pleased! But ... He had to chide me for both the choice of motif and the beautiful way in which I had painted it. In his eyes, it would have been better had I used one to undermine the other – something I had indeed done in the two paintings, but alas, apparently not to his satisfaction.

The remonstration came as little surprise as I'd already heard of a comment going around to the effect that

"Loomsden" is an absolutely fantastic painter but never in a million years should such a talent be wasted on that subject matter. What did surprise me was that he took pains to tell me at all – and in such a kind and earnest manner, as I was more used to reserved silence. I am still grateful to him for that.

The fact that B admired my ability and loathed what I did with it led me to again question my subject matter, my motifs – why I paint what I paint – and it prompted the beginnings of a discussion in my notebooks and on my laptop.

My artist colleague hadn't actually been able to help with regard to what might be "appropriate" subject matter. When I asked him facetiously what he'd have painted instead, he was stumped.

What indeed? I could see with the shift of his gaze to faraway internal shores that he was really racking his brains, but after a few moments of reflection he admitted that he had no idea, just "not that".

No doubt he'd later feed something into his computer programme and come up with a comprehensive set of instructions for proceeding.

Perhaps we should have swapped places for a while, me with his methods, he with mine. But it didn't come to that. So I continued to ponder my preferences and processes for arriving at motifs – and still do today.

The biggest problem of figurative painting is the question, what the hell should I paint?

In the studio, I encounter this dilemma on a daily basis. I have to muster the courage to go on a hunch even whilst supposing that whatever piques my interest at the time is probably a shitty idea. But I generally explore it anyway, blocking the niggling little voice of rationality because, after all, you have to get the ball rolling somehow.

Back then, talking to B about my work in the exhibition, the paintings in question were dense, hermetically sealed under toxic pink and sage-green layers with figures both human, in old fashioned costume, and animals, protagonists and bystanders in a power struggle.

Subject matter for me is less a strategic choice than a question of resonance. Why something's resonant is another matter, though perhaps it is rooted in past experiences of visual perception – so that the internal chiming of imagery can ping back and upload new meaning in the world and feed into our experience of the contemporary world afresh.

John Berger would no doubt have felt vindicated to hear that my first contact with visual art was not through an art gallery or museum (I first got to visit one of those aged seventeen) nor through reproductions in art books, which were not present on the bookshelves of our home, but through my grandma's place mats, set out under our dinner plates. They had a soft cork underbelly and a hard, smooth top like Formica on which the reproductions were printed. Gran owned several of these sets, and they were kept in the drawer of an ornate teak dresser, an unlikely piece of furniture for a council flat on the thirteenth floor of a high-rise in West Denton, Newcastle.

The sets most frequently in use depicted hunting scenes of all kinds, with not just horses and foxtails but also wild boars and lolloping wolves too. I suspect now that some of the wolf images might have been Audubon illustrations.[8] Strange to be waiting for our teas (that's dinner, if you're down south) and being drawn into a scene where wolves are issuing from their lair in the roots of an oak. Though you eat, remember, you may also be eaten.

Painting and the subject matter occurring in paintings unfolds in a continuum. What could be painted in 2021 could not be painted in 2018. What can be painted in 2015 is based on what could be painted in 2014.

I can research thematic fields for possible motifs, collect and form an image base, playfully combine imagery like a Dadaist poem or experiment with compositions in Photoshop. But all that is just preparation for the moment when I put paint on the canvas with a brush. Or a mop.

Here begins a realm that is almost impossible to put down in writing, because painting is like a wild sow dashing through the forest at a hellish pace. I ride her clinging to her back and sometimes I pull out a few of her bristles.

Painting for me is first and foremost the suspension of disbelief for subject matter, for imagery. This "suspension of disbelief", the temporary renunciation of doubt, then allows the exploration of a territory of visual relationships – without the interference of critical logic – in which structure, shape, line, pattern, proportion, colour and the relationship of individual elements to one another enter into play.

If the wild sow is really going for it, it brings me to a point in the painting where the picture stands in the studio as a kind of independent being staring me in the face. If that happens, then I'm really in.

Francis Bacon put it this way: "Real Painting is a mysterious and continuous struggle with chance. Mysterious because the very substance of the paint can make such a direct assault on the nervous system; continuous because the medium is so fluid and subtle that every change that is made loses what is already there in the hope of making a fresh gain."[9] That is why concepts make little sense in "real painting".

What's proper painting?

By now my desk is strewn with handwritten notes-to-self on the backs of envelopes: *What a pig's ear! Want to blot your copy book? Careful Lummy, don't set up your own dogma.*

So what's proper painting?

Everything actually. Cut-out painting, linear painting, neat-edged painting, dry-scrubbed painting, flat painting, layered painterly painting, messy-fatty-blob painting, thick-crusty painting, drawing-painting, painting on canvas, painting with forms, painting with forms that represent figures, painting on clay, painting on glass, painting ... well ... the whole shebang. The point is that nothing at all is contraband and even if the art industry – not just in Switzerland but everywhere – is always in the game of letting some things in and keeping other things out, you can't keep a good thing down.

And what's a good thing in painting? Like all good art, good painting leaves a trace, an after-image in the viewer that can be revisited again and again and fed upon. Good painting is often a synthesis of several qualities: The sensual-intuitive can coexist with the intellectual, and it is no problem at all to have a contemporary dialogue using an old medium like painting.

But painting's also always on the move. Think of Mark Rothko: after all his hard work, wearing his brushes down to the stumps, to make pure abstraction recognised as *the* answer to *all* painting, *everywhere*, he got severely miffed when Pop Art threw everything overboard. But, tough luck – that's the way it goes, and it's the same for us all.

And so when you open the German magazine *Spiegel* and find six pages of discourse about Sylvester Stallone's painting oeuvre, a portrait photo of old Sly with a clutch of brushes in a clenched fist, paint streaming down his forearm as if from a bloody wound sustained in battle with the Vietcong, you shouldn't be surprised: painting is, after all, a special – a very special – territory.[10]

So can I paint a tree with birds?

Course you can. In answer, I painted not just an entire rowan tree thicket full of birds, on the largest format I have, but a whole frieze of thickets over several canvases. These are paintings that dance on the retina and collapse pictorial space.

One of these large formats was hung in an exhibition and immediately ensnared art-goers in the big old bird thicket of cadmium blobs and cobalt slicks. *Thicket* was instantly sold, as was, incidentally, the very first thrush painting, which went to a wiry old lady. The masked and sanitised studio visitor, for whom beauty had been such a double-edged affair, was left out in the cold and had to arrange for another Christmas present for his parents.

The lament can still be heard, of course: Can figurative painting really be contemporary? *Eez zis wirklich* relevant now?

On a planet with 60 per cent of vertebrate creatures driven to the edge of extinction and up to half of the world's wild tree species also at risk of extinction, I'd hazard the guess ... *yes!*[11] This is why a tree with birds is rather contemporary subject matter and figurative painting just the right medium to convey it. And ta-da! There. Have your old Avant-Garde kick-in-the-shins!

2 "Die Treichler verstopfen zurzeit nicht die Intensivstationen" (The bell ringers are not currently clogging the intensive care units), interview with Christoph Blocher, Swiss SVP politician by Christina Neuhaus and Marc Tribelhorn, in *Neue Zürcher Zeitung* (*NZZ*), 16 Sep. 2021.

3 See Gregory Grämiger, Ita Heinze-Greenberg and Lothar Schmitt, *Die Schweizer Avantgarde und das Bauhaus* (The Swiss Avant-Garde and the Bauhaus), Zurich: gta Verlag, 2019.

4 From conversations with Corinne Schatz, art historian and former curator at Kunstmuseum St. Gallen, regarding the making and reception of painting in Switzerland including the example of "Paul Klee: Werke aus dem Familienbesitz" (Paul Klee: Works from the family collection), Kunstmuseum St. Gallen, 22 Jan. 1955 – 20 Mar. 1955.

5 Jennifer Dasal, "How MoMA and the CIA Conspired to Use Unwitting Artists to Promote American Propaganda During the Cold War", *Artnet*, 24 Sep. 2020, news.artnet.com/art-world/artcurious-cia-art-excerpt-1909623.

6 From conversations with Felicity Lunn, Head of Art and Design Division, Bern University of the Arts, former Director of Kunstmuseum Pasquart in Biel, Switzerland.

7 George Monbiot, "The gift we should give to the living world? Time, and lots of it", in *The Guardian*, 8 Aug. 2021.

8 John James Audubon (1785–1851) was an American artist, naturalist and ornithologist.

9 Francis Bacon explained his theory in a Tate Gallery catalogue for another artist's show, London, 1953

10 Marc Hujer, "Wer ist wichtiger, du oder der verdammte Klempner?" (Who's more important, you or the damn plumber?), in *Der Spiegel*, 49, 4 Dec. 2021.

11 See Damian Carrington, "Humanity has wiped out 60% of animal populations since 1970, report finds", in *The Guardian*, 30 Oct. 2018; Jonathan Watts, "Up to half of world's wild tree species could be at risk of extinction", in *The Guardian*, 1 Sep. 2021.

2

Pieter sends his regards – About belonging

In January 2019 a visitor to my solo show *Return of the Huntress* at Kunst(Zeug)Haus Rapperswil left an anonymous comment in the guest book: "Peter Doig lässt grüssen" (Greetings from Peter Doig). The intention of the anonymous comment was, of course, to injure and rain on the parade of a strong solo exhibition in a stunning museum by implying the work is not independent.

Greetings from Peter Doig? Not really, mate. Peel your eyes and have a better shufti.

There is another Pieter, though, to whom the title of the show refers and with whom I had often found myself in a painterly dialogue. Because with painting – as in all other art forms with a long history – someone always sends their regards: that's part of the joy of working in the continuum of painting.

That's why, dear and un-dear reader, you now are presented with a chapter on influences and the ebb and flow of currents within the sea of images.

The blazing hot moment

What interests me always and most about painting is the picture I'm currently working on. This is the frontline, where cotton-wool ear buds, the squirrel-hair brush, the floor mop, or the drying pool of turpentine stains the chalk ground. Where other paint coagulations upon untouched chalk gesso all at some point coalesce into image on canvas. There, where the paint touches the surface, at that moment, the entire history of painting is present in the bristles of the brush, pressing itself into the present. This is the blazing hot moment in painting, its urgency, its emergence on the canvas.

This is the moment I have to protect. Art catalogues remain on the shelf, painting exhibitions avoided; I don't enter other artists' studios. The picture in the coming needs its place, especially in me. This is the phase of pictorial asceticism. While looking at paintings is to be temporarily avoided, studying the sky and the weather fronts is good, as is contemplating halos of light over the village as you walk across the fields on a foggy night or watching the moon sail over the Sleeping Bishop or charting the progress of the robotic lawnmower making its lonely rounds on the darkened grounds of the dog-training club around the lamppost decked with the ramshackle storks' nest, long after everyone else has gone to bed.

When painting, the eyes need to be awake, not overfed. Once I'm painted blank, which is usually after two or three months of intensive work, I build Dora-the-crow a new enclosure or lay bricks to make a new vegetable bed. Or three. And read five urban-fantasy novels and a couple of biographies in a row. I really don't need to be bothered with art then.

Club chairs at the painters' guild

Until suddenly the hunger for images sets in and I turn almost overnight into a visual glutton. That's when I venture out again into galleries and museums to see exhibitions contemporary and historical. That's when I look through everything, no matter what, newspapers, postcards, holiday brochures, cinema posters, wallpaper-sample collections, old illustrated children's books, the puppets and figures on my cosmology shelf, historical photographs, my own photo collections, art reviews and artist interviews, people sitting in traffic jams or surreptitiously washing their armpits in the little water fountain in Zurich main station; car headlights traversing the bedroom ceiling, or the moonlight, sliced into strips by the louvre blinds, that lies in ribbons on the parquet floor. It doesn't matter what.

I throw everything in the mix regardless, painting colleagues included, contemporary and historical. I leaf through books to see how other artists solved their painterly problems ... but that's not what's important.

What is important is that they speak and use the same language as I do, and that we sit together in our heavy leather chairs in the painters' club from where there is that one very special view of the world – no matter where on the globe, no matter when in time, that eye that painters have had on the world since time immemorial and still have.

In the painters' club you'll find great-grandparent-painters, cousins, nephews, nieces, sisters, brothers. You know each other and nod to each other but keep your distance, because you know too that you can quickly trip over each other's feet, and though it's a large room, many dance.

The further away in time a member of my painting family is, the closer I can let him or her get to me.

I've been sitting next to Pieter Breughel for years now looking at his paintings in the Kunsthistorisches Museum in Vienna. No, actually, he sits down next to me, and every time I let my eye and mind travel over his paintings, I enter his penetrating gaze on the time in which he lived, feel his razor-sharp intellect, his precise emotions, sniff the air he breathed.

The "big theme" of his work trundles along incidentally, casually, understated, but its only one amongst many, not more important than the magpie on the naked winter tree or the ice skater at the back, who is taking a tumble. It is the simultaneity of everyday life and high drama in his paintings, but also the great, all-encompassing and always precise indifference of the brush, which doesn't differentiate between general and detail or between centre and edge. Everything is painted with equal skill, equal simplicity and is equally painterly. Although he's familiar with the tricks of central perspective and uses them cleverly, it is never about the one focus or the one meaning; he allows his pictures to elude the viewer, to withdraw from you, again. Perhaps that is why they are still as beautiful as they are enigmatic, even today.

I, in turn, let him know what capers and contortions people perform in front of his works these days, whether with iPad, digital camera, or audio guide. How many take passing snapshots with their mobiles held aloft as they saunter by rather than pausing in front of them to actually really look.

And then there are those who are indeed drawn into the painting's orbit, pulled closer and closer until a hidden loudspeaker barks out, "Stand back, please!" and they recoil, startled and guilty.

I tell him that for his really big show in Vienna in 2018 one had to book tickets months in advance, with quarter-hour time slots for entry, and how there are coffee mugs and beauty cases and bath towels with *Return of the Hunters* for sale in the store. He snorts at that, shrugs his shoulders – every age has its folly. In today's world, he muses, moviemaking would be exciting. Maybe.

I painted *Return of the Huntress* on a canvas more than twice the size of his painting. No exhausted men returning from a meagre hunt but a single figure carrying her bounty not into the village but into the metropolis, under the emerald green, evening sky.

So in that exhibition at Kunst(Zeug)Haus in Rapperswil, there was indeed a Pieter waving a "hello" – and duly acknowledged in the title of the exhibition. No, not Peter Doig, ya great numpty – Pieter Breughel the Elder!

The conversation among painters of different centuries flows easily and freely because the medium of painting and its fundamentals – pigment, binder, painting support, application – have hardly changed.

Francis Bacon spoke to Velásquez, Titian and Van Gogh; I speak with him but also with Breughel, Turner, Sickert, Beckmann, Nash, Vanessa Bell, Gwen John, Jessica Dismorr, Alice Neel, Malcolm Morley ... and many more. You also encounter your contemporary cousins too – like Joan Mitchell, Fiona Ray, Michael Armitage, Karen Kilimnik, Lynette-Yiadom Boakye, Dana Schutz, Marlene Dumas, Henry Taylor, Cecily Brown and, of course, Peter Doig. There are a few long lost and greatly missed Aunties, too, like Maria Lassnig and Rose Wylie – not known to me in my formative student years but estranged only because they hadn't been properly introduced. Everyone, really everyone, engaged in the strands of this great overlapping conversation.

This painter's view of the world no matter where on the globe, no matter when in history, is "painterly". "Painterly", not in the "quaint" sense but in the sense of it being embedded in the quantum physical fold between matter and representation, in which a spot of colour can be simultaneously both cadmium red blobs and a cluster of rowan berries.

And really, that is one of the big joys of painting: you belong to a huge family and are never alone. But, as is the case with every family, you have to live your own life too.

Uncle Walter

In 2018 I met the late, greatly missed Delphine Lévy, then Director of Museums in Paris, who curated the first comprehensive retrospective of the work of the British painter Walter Sickert in mainland Europe, in Dieppe in 2015. With a smile, she told me that she had recently come across the catalogue *Rachel Lumsden – Return of the Huntress* in the bookshop of the Tate Modern in London; now she was keen to meet the artist and view her work in person, which was why she was attending my exhibition preview in Paris.

It was not Pieter Breughel we were talking about then but about Walter Sickert, as a major influence on painting in Britain even today. Ms Lévy declared me to be a metaphorical descendant, sharing an unashamed love affair with painting, its clashes and clangs with representation.

We talked about atmosphere in his work, of temperature, weather and mood, of urban motif and the condensed, almost curdled impasto quality of paint on the canvas – an uncomfortable grittiness and pressing materiality through which every dirty little secret of city life is made evident. We spoke of the generally tightly held tonality of his palette used with such restraint that a pale-orange shopfront or a bruised violet sky jump out with jarring effect – a visual play with the viewer ensuring psychological consequences.

Around Christmas 2021, I received a request from Paris to print my painting *Mr Wolf* in the context of a text Delphine Lévy had written shortly before her sudden death in 2020. *Mr Wolf* was to appear in the catalogue accompanying the major Sickert retrospective at the Petit Palais in Paris in 2022.[12] The request touched me very much and, of course, I said yes.

So now I hold this brick of a book in my lap and leaf through: Sickert's works, those of his predecessors, his peers, his descendants. I see the rise and fall of the conversation across the generations and find myself, without effort, sitting again in the club chairs watching the dancers in this painting story. The usual suspects of the London School are all present: Freud, Bacon, Auerbach, Kossoff, but also Hockney, Hopper, Blake (Peter), Paula Rego, Cecily Brown, Lynette-Yiadom Boakye. The fact that my name and my work are also among them not only makes me quiver with joy, it also triggers a kind of happy refrain in my brain: *Who the fuck is Rachel Lumsden?* Well, she's a painter amongst other painters.

After half a lifetime as a painter and a considerable number of years as a lecturer and advocate of painterly figuration in my own right, I can now sometimes catch a glimpse of my own little legacy, as Auntie or older sister to some of the younger generation of painters, especially here in Switzerland, former students and mentees; colleagues are also among them. My work too has become part of the canon for a new generation of painters – and so it is possible to encounter the occasional comment that this work or that looks like a Loomsden and I think, great, stuff is being handed on, so that *Rachel Lumsden lässt grüssen* too, as one amongst others.

12 Delphine Lévy, *Sickert: La provocation et l'énigme*, Paris: Cohen&Cohen Éditeurs, 2021.

3

The gallery – A crash course in dealing with the auxiliary force

A lot can be said about galleries, gallerists and art dealers, but the main point is simple: with a good gallery, both the work and life of an artist are made easier.

Henry

My first gallerist in London was a huge, broad man in his early sixties with a penchant for floral shirts and kaftans and a skin that looked permanently sunburnt. Let's call him Henry. He had read a big article in the *Independent* newspaper in 1998 about the graduating exhibition of all the London Art-MAs. Not only had the critic reviewed my work there, but the accompanying generous photo spread had also shown Lumsden in her studio in front of one of her 3-metre-high paintings.

Henry offered me a solo show in his small but busy gallery in Shoreditch, a neighbourhood which teetered on the edge of a great boom in the late nineties, having previously been colonised by artists in need of cheap studios and living space. In the meantime, banks and big business were already muscling in and a lot of money was spilling out of the nearby City, London's financial district, into the markets, including that of the art trade.

This was a time of many emerging galleries, all keen to get in on the art scene. We're not talking about old-school gallerists like Leo Castelli, who paid the artists he had under contract an annual salary for exclusive access to their work, whether the work sold or not. Neither are we really talking about a model with a fair distribution of labour in return for a share of the proceeds – oh no. A lot of people at the time thought that selling art was an easy way to make a lot of money, and that providing exhibition space was enough to pocket 50 per cent and upwards of the turnover – without any further obligations, no strings attached. Henry was not like that. He had moved to London from New York because he loved the London gay scene, was generally an anglophile and had both a good eye for quality and a great affinity for painting. I liked him.

The art market is a classic "people's business" where the interpersonal is as important as the art itself. An art dealer is successful when she makes it possible for a collector to embark on the same journey of discovery with the artworks that she has previously made herself. She listens, stays in the background, creates the space in which collector and works can get to know each other. She speaks little – but when she does, then with precision, with knowledge and at the right time. She can also gauge if and why the collector is interested, whether it's a single purchase or the building up of an existing collection, and she will bring works or groups of works to view accordingly.

Henry, on the other hand, was a windbag who, after a sentence or two about the work, became obsessed with only one subject – himself. As a visitor to the gallery, one ran first and foremost into the many hundreds of pages of his biography, *The Life and Times of Henry R*, and should one actually have made it to the last page of this weighty tome and not have been swept from the gallery by the torrent of words, one was allowed to look at the art. To my great astonishment, despite his incessant first-person narration, he actually occasionally sold works – not in large numbers and rarely the large formats; nevertheless, that was a great help to me at the time.

You have to know that nobody, really *nobody*, in the UK is waiting for another art school graduate wannabe, even if she comes along out of one of the more prestigious postgraduate London art schools. You have to know that compared to the solid, well-organised Swiss arts funding, there are at best trace elements of public funding in the UK, tiny sums of money that all thirty-seven thousand officially recognised artists are fighting pointlessly over. In other words, far too many are jockeying for one tiny crumb of cake. Heated studio? *Njet*, forget it. Running water? Not unless you count the leaky roof dripping into a bucket. I was glad that I could work in a junk room where the windows weren't smashed and the door had a good lock with an entryway that wasn't doubling as a public lavatory and place to shoot up.

So manna falls from heaven when you not only get a solo exhibition with a decently printed invitation card in a trendy gallery in Shoreditch but can also sell a few small works of art.

When I was invited to group shows at another gallery, however, Henry objected.

Now, group exhibitions are important for artists for two reasons: first, you rub shoulders with your peers, meeting like-minded professional colleagues and second, they bring different and greater audiences to your work than you could ever possibly manage under your own steam. If in addition your large-format paintings are also shown to advantage in a bright and airy gallery space, it is almost a duty to accept such an invitation.

But Henry saw it differently: he insisted that I could only exhibit with him, although there was no exclusive contract between us that would have given him the sole right to show my work. Had he organised additional and larger exhibitions in other spaces, that would not have been a problem for me, but Henry dug in and insisted that everything should revolve entirely around his small gallery in *R-Lane*. This was a dead end for my paintings and we eventually parted ways. He refused to return or pay me for works that he still had in storage and thus ended our working relationship with pilfering.

Normally, a gallery likes to represent the complete works of an artist. In my particular case that would mean paintings in large and small formats, monotypes and drawings. The focus would clearly be on painting, so the infrastructure of the gallery would have to be suitable for that above all. This applies not only to the actual exhibition space but also to the storage area where the gallery keeps works available for sale when not exhibited. Additionally, the gallery's infrastructure also includes its professional expertise, its client base, the publication of catalogues of works, participation in national and international art fairs, contacts with the media, the maintenance of a representative website and the use of social media.

A "good" gallery allows the artist to concentrate on her work. The gallery brings the work to the public and secures a place for it there with regular exhibitions in the gallery and at art fairs, with sales to museums and public collections. It thus not only provides the artist with a financial base but also helps her build her reputation.

A "good" artist, in turn, not only regularly supplies the gallery with new works of consistent quality, but also contributes to the gallery's good reputation with her career. It should be self-evident that both sides abide by the contract they have agreed: the artist does not sell works behind the gallery's back, thus cheating it out of its fair share of the profits and the gallery settles accounts with the artist regularly, cleanly and correctly.

One can see that the interaction between the artist and the gallery is ideally a long-term relationship towards a common goal from which both parties have mutual benefit.

Both are rewarded with a steady increase in status, reach and sales prices.

Bianca

After Henry, there were various group shows and a few solo shows in *off-spaces* before the collaboration with another commercial gallery in London got underway. The gallery owner – let's call her Bianca – had roots both in London and Milan and regularly commuted between the two cities. She was in her mid-thirties, *Tatler* chic, and once a week gave her lustrous hair an overnight soak in olive oil, which she highly recommended. That was one of the few details of personal information to be gleaned from her; she had nothing in common with Henry in this respect.

Bianca, though, also kept her views on art to herself, which was no problem for me because the gallery space was beautiful, bright and spacious, and Bianca's exhibitions featured a catchy mix of interesting artists of quality.

Things were going well until Bianca showed signs of unreliability. For instance, I managed to get a *Guardian* art critic interested in a two-person show at Bianca's gallery. You can imagine my disappointment when the angry journalist let it be known that she had twice stood in front of locked gallery doors during the official opening hours. Of course, nothing came of the article. I found this enormously frustrating, not only because of the missed review in the *Guardian*, which could have been both a valuable and effective help, but because I was already living in Switzerland at the time and it had been quite a feat to get the big works to London in the first place.

Although Bianca's gallery was spacious, bright and ideal for painting, there were hardly any sales because she was testing a new business model: *art leasing*. Collectors no longer bought the works but borrowed them as "clients" for a fixed monthly rate.

Art leasing is ideal for people who view their walls as a kind of enlarged TV screen and who prefer to zap through art instead of hopping TV channels. Good for them, but for the artist on the other end of the deal it was a different kettle of fish. On the one hand, the works were blocked for months on end for little monetary return; on the other, they were often taken out of storage, transported, hung up and taken down with little care so that they showed scratches and scuff marks. In addition, gallery storage in a damp depot made the canvases saggy and exposed them to mould.

Fellow artists also represented by Bianca began to speculate on the lack of sales in the gallery. Although no one seemed to be selling much and the income from art leases was small, the gallery was never short of money, despite the enormous fixed costs that location and size entailed. It was well known that there were businesses in London that laundered money under the guise of normal activity and therefore it did not need a fertile imagination to speculate in this direction. Whether that was the case with Bianca or not was impossible to tell. My relationship with the gallery gradually dwindled over time without any actual break – and that was fine with me. However, mindful of my experience with Henry, I made sure I had my work back first.

The commercial art gallery dominates the middle tier of the art market and functions in principle as an intermediary between the artist and the collector, whether in the private or institutional sectors, i.e. museums.

In a society based on the division of labour, a "good" gallery takes over marketing, distribution and sales. This should in no way be confused with patronage: the connection between artist and gallery is not a matter of benefaction or sponsorship, but a business relationship in which the artist as producer and the gallery owner as distributor split the proceeds, usually fifty-fifty.

Heidi

After living in eastern Switzerland for a while, a gallery owner – let's call her Heidi – invited me to her space for a talk. We agreed on a date, I would bring my portfolio, we would talk about the work and find out if we could do business together.

The idiosyncrasies and codes of art communities are inevitably influenced by the prevailing cultural elements of time and place and so differ all over the world. Before I came to London in the nineties, I had half-dreaded my relocation to the metropolis where everything, including the art scene would, I assumed, be less familial, harder and more aggressive. To my surprise, the London art world at that time seemed almost village-like.

Back then, the galleries were concentrated in the West End, on Cork Street behind the Royal Academy and the small roads criss-crossing Bond Street, so the scene was accessible. On Friday evenings, people moved from one preview to the next; the good-humoured mix of art and wine was rarely interrupted by speeches. One also saw the direct chatting up of curators, dealers and critics by young artists as a natural part of the exchange. This relatively new convention had a great deal to do with the success of the YBAs (the Young British Artists, or Brit-pack) who shot to prominence in the late eighties and early nineties, with the help of young German-British art dealer Karsten Schubert, ushering in a new relationship between artists, dealers and curators of the scene. Regarding this new art etiquette and the YBAs, Schubert commented: "The classic pattern had been that you were watched by dealers for a while and got an occasional studio visit and pat on the back. ... These artists were not willing to play the game that way. They wanted to change the rules and take the initiative."[13]

The new rules were a matter of course for students of art like me, who benefited from a less rigid approach within the art scene, but they did not prepare me well for my entry into the Swiss art world a few years later where it seemed one had to play the shy creature, demurely waiting to be deer-stalked and discovered amongst the art foliage by keen-eyed art explorers. I was completely unaware of this until a fellow artist from St. Gallen scolded me in tones both imploring and exasperated, admonishing me to keep my trap shut when in the noble company of curators and similar art honourees and, crucially, to speak only when spoken to unless I wanted to ruin my chance of ever being lifted up and kissed awake.

Perhaps it helps the reader to know that my move to Switzerland had been a little bit bumpy. A visual artist with her core interest in painterly figuration, a *painter's painter,* who had somewhat stubbornly and with a lot of commitment slowly made her way at least to the fringes of the art world in London; in Switzerland, on the other hand, had turned overnight into one of the many doctors' wives who had chosen painting as a hobby. My request to exhibit locally in the off-space earned only hilarity and derision. This would rattle around my brain at night as I lay awake in bed, a nagging riddle along the lines of an English Christmas-cracker joke with just as naff a punch-line: "What d'ya get if you cross a figurative painter with a doctor's wife? Frau Doktor Hobby Painter."

I had as little use for the role of hobby-painting doctor's wife as I did for that of a wallflower on the local art scene, which seemed to me to be organised like a lesson in a dance school. *Bollocks to that.*

That and a few other factors put so much pressure on the marriage that my Swiss husband and I suddenly found ourselves under the storm clouds of divorce. Such intriguing society news travels quickly in the relevant social classes and is obviously important, but I was neither aware of the fact nor could I imagine that it could play a role in the art world. Hmm.

In the meantime, I put together a portfolio for the meeting with gallery owner Heidi, and hoped for a professional conversation followed by the chance of a studio visit. But no sooner had I entered the gallery, Heidi, trim in a twinset and pearls way, immediately and brusquely sent me away on the grounds that she had no time. The fact that her behaviour, devoid of all politeness, was evidently unusual could be seen in the face of the gallery assistant.

We both stared at each other in amazement and neither of us could make sense of the brusque refusal nor the equally brusque stalking away of the gallery owner to the back rooms, slamming the door and leaving me – her invited guest – standing with my portfolio like a refused foundation course applicant. Still befuddled by the odd meeting, I later heard the rumour that news of my impending divorce had rendered me, in Heidi's eyes, into a singularly uninteresting prospect, as the expectation of sales to beautify the walls of the doctor's surgery – not just the husband's but those of all his colleagues – had collapsed. The Little Painter without a buyer's base was in Heidi's eyes nothing but that: a little painter.

That was my first encounter with an art speculation in which the art itself played no role.

Art dealers and gallery owners usually have their own collectors' base, although they very much welcome an artist bringing her own buyers into the show. Artists also recognise that it is advantageous to invite their collectors because it gives more weight to the artist in the eyes of the gallery.

I had colleagues in London who, when they were able to participate in a group show at a coveted gallery, would get their friends to pose as collectors and buy a small work or two incognito, thus increasing their standing and getting the gallery to include them in their programme on a permanent basis. Once or twice, I too have assisted in such an operation and found it fascinating to be on the other side of the financial equation and to realize how differently one is greeted and perceived when one appears with a briefcase in hand. Bringing a painting into an exhibition as an artist and taking one out as a collector, are two different worlds.

The art world is vast and global, no longer confined to the major metropolises. Therefore galleries, like publishers, develop their own particular niche-profile in the market. Many galleries are concerned with the primary market – i.e. the work of living artists. Some galleries are focused on the secondary market – work from prior periods on the art timeline as well as the resale of well-established living artists – and some "blue-chip" galleries span both primary and secondary markets mostly with prominent, best-selling names and prices that do not generally lose value over time because enough people are investing. Additionally, there are further subdivisions based on medium (painting, sculpture, new media, etc.) or a mixture of mediums – and ultimately the expertise and preferences of the art dealer will be the deciding factor.

The primary market is more speculative than the other markets because contemporary artists do not yet have the benefit of retrospective evaluation, i.e. the rubber stamp ultimately sealing unequivocal approval often falls with the scythe.

However, this can also be an extremely lucrative market as essentially the *ultra contemporary* young artists can be cheaper initially so if you hoover up works good and early you might be lucky and hit the jackpot.

Other factors in a work's status include the artist's growing reputation and past success, as measured by her experience and consistency of artistic practice in terms of quality and aesthetics. Critical evaluation and opinions given by art historians and art experts; art-school training, inclusion in respected art magazines and catalogues; inclusion in group and solo exhibitions, inclusion in exhibitions within museums or equivalent institutions. All these aspects influence the rank an artist receives within rating systems, as practised, for example, by the Swiss Institute for Art Research with its online encyclopaedia of Swiss artists "Sikart".

The career I had begun prior to coming to Switzerland, including a handful of solo and group shows in London as well as in the city museum of Nottingham, with accompanying reviews from the *Independent*, *Guardian*, *Evening Standard* and *Time Out* and inclusion in a museum catalogue, turned out not to count for much when arriving in Switzerland, and the career dial was returned to zero.

Johann

After some difficult years, I was delighted in 2005 to receive funding for a project from the cultural department of the city of St. Gallen. In the wake of this wonderful happening, a gallery owner offered me an exhibition. Of course I was thrilled and more than happy to accept the offer, but later my eyes widened when he – let's call him Johann – sent a contract to be signed, which would not only grant him the exclusive right of disposal over all my work – including my entire back catalogue of paintings from year dot – but also entitled him to a share of every *Kunst am Bau* (art for architecture) commission, with or without his contribution to such a project.

Johann, who with elegant chiselled profile and fine skull resembled one of the Helvetic founding fathers in the Hodler fresco *Unanimity* (1911–13), had previously worked in finance, and apparently knew very well about favourable terms and conditions but had less idea about what makes artists tick.

Comparing the contract he'd presented me with the standard contracts as signed by fellow artists, I found that some of those specifications were rather unusual. So I drafted a contract in English along the lines of those of my colleagues. It assured him his 50 per cent share of sales for works exhibited in the gallery and all works created during our term of contract, initially beginning with a one-year period but with an option to extend.

On his side he would host my works in exhibitions in his gallery and the art fairs he was engaged in. Johann was a bit miffed, and accused me of having consulted a lawyer – he obviously didn't credit me with enough intelligence to be able to think and formulate for myself, even in my own native language – but he accepted.

It is worthwhile for artists outside Switzerland to know that their Swiss colleagues have the considerable clout of the artists' association Visarte behind them, which robustly represents their interests on a political and social level, a sort of union advocating fair conditions for artistic practice and offering advice to artists on everything from contracts to copyright, from social security to securing fair fees for exhibitions in art institutions.

The exhibition at Johann's gallery went rather well with an enjoyable and well-attended opening. There were a few sales and a good review in the local press. But Johann did not take my work to the art fairs, as he did with the works of the other artists he represented – even though he had contractually agreed to do so. When I asked him why, it came out that during my absence he had invited a representative of the local art museum to the exhibition to assess my potential. And that dude, with a couple of spuds for eyes when it came to figurative painting, gave the thumbs down and classified me as at best of local interest. Ergo, no representation at art fairs, no participation in further group exhibitions.

In response to my objections and evident disappointment, Johann announced that his gallery was the best thing that ever could happen to somebody like me, that if I thought I could do any better for myself, then I would have to think again. Had it really escaped me that the world was littered with second-rate artists?

Well, slice it how you will, Johann had not only shown me his *Ostschweizer* version of the proverbial "glass ceiling", the invisible barrier to women's upward mobility, but had also put me into his own personal, solidly Helvetic, reinforced concrete bunker. The fact that I did not renew the contract with him probably needs no further explanation.

On finding oneself in a paternalistic relationship of this kind, however, it is important to examine the role one has assumed in the equation and to ask whether one's own behaviour à la damsel-in-distress, has contributed to it. Looking back on it today, I cannot completely dismiss this as – at the beginning of my time in what was then a new and confusing country – I would actually have been happy to receive guidance and support. The role of the damsel in distress, however, is degrading and damaging because it involves the constant appeasement of an art daddy who even likes to think he steers his young protégée to better work, often quite literally by telling her to remove this shape here or that one there. She in turn is required to simper and say how right he was and how the painting is much, much better as a result. I don't think so. Therefore: Thanks but no thanks.

After the separation from Johann, I was fed up for a while and turned down offers from other galleries. Nothing very exciting of course: a would-be gallerist met me at his space with a smearing of paste around his mouth, waving a tuna sandwich in his hand as he tried and failed to remember the names of the artists he was showing or to say anything of interest about the work. Another put more emphasis on the *Apéro riche* in their online programme than on the work they showed.

Thanks guys, but really no thank you.

Sand grain and mother of pearl

It can seem like something of a cliché to talk about *sand in the oyster*, the idiom that declares adverse conditions in the form of irritants to the system – the grain of sand – to be the key ingredient for the formation of a pearl.

But at this juncture I had to stop and ask myself a few questions: Did I need this constant resistance? Was I in need of my own friction surface, a cheese grater, if you will, to grate my cheese against?

I think I was. I attempted to adapt both my work and myself. If you can't show painting in the local project space, oh well never mind, make a couple of videos instead. If messy, gloopy painting doesn't cut the mustard, pare it down, make it more hard-edged. If you want to rub shoulders with other artists and get to know what makes the local scene tick, volunteer as an organiser/curator/general dogsbody at said off-space. Stay for a fairytale seven-year stint organising exchange exhibitions and film nights between your off-space and similar projects in your land of origin. Write texts about the work of the artists exhibiting in the language you are still trying to learn and present these texts in public on the opening nights of exhibitions (ignore amused twittering at mispronounced umlauts). Hand out beer from behind the bar and wash the glasses. If you can't apply for a grant without a concept, invent a project that doesn't constrict you but can still be sold as a concept. If your painting falls on blind eyes, try the ears: talk about it, why you make it, what kind of keyhole it offers and to where.

The learning curve was steep. If I hadn't thought that staying and making the effort would pay off at some point, I would have flicked the V's at the whole thing and been on my way. It was my decision to stay. Surely optimism and hope were involved, the belief in progress, the belief in the possibility of cracking the code, the hope of eventually belonging. The resistance in Switzerland shaped me and my work and also led me to reflect and ask questions that I might never have asked myself had I stayed in Britain.

Of course, it is not only friction that gives rise to change and development. The grain of sand is indeed the nucleus of the pearl, but it is the nacre-balsam that the oyster secretes and which, as mother-of-pearl, is deposited layer upon layer around the grain of sand that forms the pearl. In Switzerland, it is the funding institutions that make their own patented nacre available to the artist, with a comprehensive and far-reaching system of support, with Pro Helvetia, the arts council for Switzerland, at the national level, the cantonal administration for art and culture at regional, county level, and the city administration for art and culture at municipal level. These arts administrative bodies are looking to support artists of quality and potential but they function independently of the programmes and rules written in the museums, *Kunsthallen* and off-spaces.

In St. Gallen, this triad of museum, *Kunsthalle* and off-space seemed to operate like three levels of a single chain of command: none of them even wanted to look at my work. It was the public funding institutions that fortunately created a counterweight here. The extraordinary generosity of the city and cantonal arts administration bodies of St. Gallen, then later that of the art administration body of Thurgau, transformed those early years in Ostschweiz for me as a painter. These bodies do not just hand out financial grants but afford the grantees high visibility, through exhibition opportunities and by sounding the gong for each year's group of chosen artists in the form of laudations at a prize-giving ceremony. The financial part of the award enables artists to realise new works, but perhaps most important of all is the demonstrative act of recognition for the artist and the declaration of confidence in the quality of the work she produces. Such a support system reflects a wider general attitude, namely that artists are worth having, culture is worth supporting.

To contrast with Britain, where little funding exists for individual artists, one is more likely to encounter the general view that artists, outside of those who have succeeded to an indisputable level (and who pay correspondingly sizeable amounts of tax) are scroungers and layabouts.

But cantonal and city support for artists in Switzerland also provides subsidised studio spaces, artist residencies abroad, financial support for work catalogues – all of which affords local artists a legitimised and professional standing in their immediate environment, even if it far from guarantees cross-regional, national, or even local success in the parallel world of art institutions, the museums, off-spaces and *Kunsthallen*.

This is an exceptional system of promotion of and support for artists, the like of which I have never experienced before anywhere else. And the most extraordinary thing of all was that they unquestionably accepted me as one of their own.

One of the reasons why I suddenly belonged not only to St. Gallen but also to the canton of Thurgau was the move of my studio in 2010 first to an old machinery factory, then to a former boat workshop of the harbour master of Arbon, a small town on Lake Constance. Without realising it, I had crossed a cantonal border in the process. There out in the sticks, far away from the *St. Galler* art scene, I was able to return to my painting roots. I painted deep into the night, in winters when the lakeshore froze and sang like cut glass, in summers too when it resounded in many voices from the nearby swimming pool. I experienced a more benevolent eye on my painting and allies began to appear. It was also a time when curators who had previously quite adamantly rejected my work changed their minds: "*Doch, doch*, these paintings have ... something." Of course, I had also adapted, and my work with me. I had become more permeable, but still remained a painter to my boots.

On Friday evenings, I returned to St. Gallen earlier than usual to sing in the church choir, my hair still smelling of turpentine and linseed oil. After rehearsing Bruckner's *Te Deum* or Mozart's Requiem – or whatever had been chosen for the Easter Mass – we would go to a bar together. I heard stories from long-gone childhood days, when beech leaves were collected in the forest on warm, windy *föhn* days for stuffing the mattress or of au-pairing in Churchill's Downing Street household, as a fellow soprano had done as a young woman. At the annual choir party I learned Swiss folk songs about the girl who didn't want to marry the poor farmer's son, and of the mustering of many songbirds, blackbird, thrush, finch and starling, and I loved it.

A few years later at the ceremony at the university of St. Gallen in which I received my Swiss citizenship, I suddenly found tears pricking my eyes, much to my consternation. Perhaps because of the national anthem, which I had learned on YouTube, a yearning, melodious sonnet to the landscape ... Or was it the speech of the city's president, in which he urged us not forget our roots but to bring the richness of our diverse backgrounds with us for re-launch in our new homeland. "Thank you", I thought. "I will", as I rummaged in my satchel for a Kleenex. Later, I waited on the platform at the train station, still full of wonder about what I had just experienced, especially when I compared it with the approaching Brexit in Great Britain, which had just rudely showed its closest friends and allies the door. During the train ride in the Voralpenexpress from St. Gallen via Rapperswil, the Seedamm, the high moor of Rothenturm, down to Arth-Goldau and on to Lake Lucerne, where a huge panorama of the Alps unfolded, I understood that the magic and ecstasy of Switzerland lay in its landscape, while its urban rationality was at home in the cities. The trains of the Swiss railroads shuttle back and forth between them deep into the night when they appear to be but meandering ribbons of brightly glowing lozenges in the darkness.

It spoke for Johann that several years later, at an art prize-giving ceremony, when I had had some international solo exhibitions in respectable art institutions, had received international art prizes as well as cantonal ones and had apparently made it without him, a few rungs above the level he had predicted for me, that he later personally acknowledged my success and told me he was pleased to see that I had made my way after all. "Blimey," I thought, "and if he hadn't needed to play the art chaperone we would have gotten quite a bit higher faster."

Because this, dear reader – if I may address you directly in the traditional literary way – you must believe: always trying to do things under your own steam is such a chore. That is why a good gallery owner who knows and grasps his or her profession is always very welcome.

Now, before you start thinking that the world of galleries is populated only by windbags, dark horses, paternalistic guardians, or sharp speculators, let me assure you that this is not the case – even if the art market tends to produce precisely such types. Apart from an artist's existence, running a gallery is probably one of the most precarious careers unless one has ample private means and/or access to wealthy and eager collectors. The prestigious, international milieu of art fairs, where not only the highest sales are made but where one also meets the most important museum curators, remains closed to small fry. Should such a gallery minnow actually manage to get through the vetting, he or she is likely to be lucky to make back the investment on the booth. Those with high prices and the best names also attract the big money and can pay the booth fee out of the petty cash box. The art market is one of those *Winner Takes All* constructs, which we have become so terribly familiar with in society in general ....

These days I work with several galleries at the same time – and do it with pleasure. All of us are respectful of one another and the contribution we make to our joint endeavour; all of us love painting. We are not bound by contracts. None of us belongs to the blue-chip high flyers, with the regrettable disadvantage that the prestigious art fairs are not open to us. This nomadic life between a gallery in Paris, a small gallery in London and a regional gallery in Arbon, makes me feel fortunate, because all three places are opportunities to show my paintings. They bring my work to their client bases; in turn, I bring my collectors to their galleries. It's a *ménage à quatre*, with people so balanced and unafraid who trust their own eyes and accept strong painting as much as other art forms, that it's easy to consent to being travellers together, sustaining and helping each other.

If you are a gallery owner and believe you fit this profile *and* are passionate about your work, please feel free to contact me. To everyone else, I continue to wish you all the best and continued enjoyable reading!

13 Charles Darwent, "Karsten Schubert obituary", in *The Guardian*, 1 Aug. 2019.

4

Art beasties – A bestiary of art deciders

In Johann's gallery, a powerful Art Decider had once made a judgement about my paintings, which dropped a steel shutter in front of my work. In Johann's eyes, this judgement not only excluded me from participating in art fairs and group exhibitions, it also made it impossible for my art to be shown in the institutions in that Art Decider's domain.

Regardless of where in the world, the influence of Art Deciders and experts is of enormous importance: they determine and enforce what kind of art counts in their domain. These are the chairpersons running the show who are well networked with their international colleagues, with cultural politicians, cultural journalists, collectors, auction houses ... They determine which artists will be shown in the institution under their control in the coming years, if not decades, and, implicitly and inevitably, which will not.

Of course, these illustrious well-educated personages have both the right and the mandate to shape the field – and do so with gusto. For a director-curator is not a passive creature, but shapes art at least as much as the art-makers do, simply because the Art Decider generally has a much greater sphere of influence than an artist: so in selecting, gathering and regrouping the "fruits" of art for public consumption, they are among the most important cultural influencers and trendsetters, with a firm hand on the cultural tiller.

At art school one learnt that the structure and order of the art world has been in place since forever, or pretty much since the first troglodytes carved cudgels for belladonna berries. The quicker you come to terms with that, the less trouble and grief you will have trying to play the art world.

Imagine a sort of snakes-and-ladders game. Each field is a segment of the art scene: a commercial gallery, a non-profit off-space, a museum – and, in the sexy continental version, a *Kunsthalle*. There are programmes of education, curators, movers and shakers in the form of art writers, critics and other experts. As with snakes and ladders, you don't necessarily have to plod diligently through every stop on the way but can make use of some of the ladders to get higher faster. There are some pitfalls, however, that can plunge you down the scaly back of a snake – so watch out.

The optimistic advice in my student years was that those who figured out the nature of the system could swing swiftly from ladder to ladder in the art jungle and get to where the big bananas hang.

I like the image of the artist as a skilful chimp who, thanks to her supple arms, shimmies from exhibition to exhibition, gallery to gallery, museum to museum – as if her career were orderly and predictable, as if nothing happened by chance or was influenced by luck. Art institutions, museums and galleries have the most excellent reasons for showing the artists they choose, whose careers have progressed step by step and are pursued with determination and resolve, i.e. heave-ho, lads and lasses, and you'll get there in the end. Or not.

When I look back at myself walking down Multergasse in St. Gallen in the early noughties, on my way to an opening or an artist talk at the museum, the *Kunsthalle* or the offspace ExEx, hoping to meet people and find allies in a hitherto unfamiliar art scene, I see my former self as if in a TV re-enactment of a crime. Should I warn the plucky little painter to turn around right now and return home while she still can? Because in eastern Switzerland figurative painting doesn't even register on the art barometer – because she lacks any understanding of what it will mean for her to work here. That in the moment she professes to paint, long before she has even unpacked her wares, she will be declaring herself a leper – she has no idea of the codes and invisible barriers of the local art gang.

Should I warn her? But she doesn't slow down, just gives me a smile. It's then that I can return the grin and give her a nod: "Go on then, Lummy, if you must. You always want to do it the hard way and you can have that here just as much as in London." Off she goes, full of confidence towards the Museumsquartier ready for battle with the big beasts.

It is now worth taking a closer look at the species of Art Deciders, in order to describe and catalogue the mythical creatures one may encounter in the vastness of the art tundra. Let's start with the Constant Gardeners.

The Constant Gardeners[14]

They are characterised by their deep and open conception of art which, although shaped by training and experience, is not inflexible. Constant Gardeners have no need to play different art forms off against each other which means that painting, even the figurative variety, is just as naturally a contemporary means of expression as a video installation. Of course, they too have preferences, but they are always evolving, and rightly so, because Art itself is a roving creature, as likely to double back on itself and pick up a forgotten scent as it is to continue forever on a straight and rigid course.

Their Gardens are the interface between artist, institution and public sphere. It depends on the institution and the region in which the Constant Gardener works, whether the different genres of art coexist simultaneously or one after the other in separate individual or thematically curated group exhibitions. The discussion about the legitimacy of painting with the Constant Gardeners is superfluous from the very beginning. Decisive for them is the strength of a position, its quality and intention and the developmental arc of the work as a whole.

For the Little Painter this is great, for she herself is in flux, developing new interests, new muscles and loves nothing more than when she is encouraged to grow and can take on new challenges.

A second quality that Constant Gardeners share is their willingness to visit the artist in the studio or at her exhibition to initiate a conversation about the work. This implies a direct encounter with the work and real looking, thinking and articulating. Because this species of Art Decider is driven by curiosity and the need for growth for themselves and others, they don't wait until they retire to see an artist's work first-hand. Although they too scrutinise an artist's résumé to see if it is graced by any prestigious exhibitions in renowned institutions, they assess the quality and developmental potential of an artist in the context of an ongoing and personal exchange with her and her works. Because even the Constant Gardeners are seeking nourishment for themselves and their institution, which in turn is enriching for their art public.

I am thinking in particular of a representative of this species who has a wonderfully easy way of dealing with the painter's intellect and appreciates her thoughts and insights to such an extent that, visiting the studio, he opens his notebook and takes notes on her theories and explanations. To colleagues present who drop a quizzical comment, he explains with a chuckle that one can never know when one will have to write the next laudation or need a clever sentence for a lecture on painting, and that this painter, in particular, knows how to express herself once she gets going.

Once things have developed to the point of being offered a solo exhibition, a Constant Gardener never needs simply to fill their exhibition rooms, but wants to curate exhibitions together with the artist, finding new connections for the work within the context of the space. Of course, she has already developed ideas about sequences and rhythms in the arrangement of the paintings, has noted the work groups appropriate to this space or that, has considered contrasts and opposing positions, thought up themes for individual rooms. In other words, it is easy for a Constant Gardener to create a painterly "film" for her rooms. But this is not yet set in absolute terms, and instead this vision is offered to the painter as a partner on an equal footing. A dialogue develops in which the proposal is tested and discussed before a decision is made, and the painter learns new things about her own work.

Such a Constant Gardener also knows about the unspectacular, solid work that has to be done behind the scenes. She submits applications for funding to the relevant offices and regional supporters well in advance of the exhibition; this has become second nature to her due to long experience and common sense.

The per diems that the artist receives for her time working on the exhibition are also paid without discussion. More important for the artist, however, is the gain in historicity, namely the fact that her works and her name are linked to the museum's lines of tradition. The conversation offered by the Constant Gardener is also the point at which the artist's new groups of works are included in the contemporary art discourse. It is an enormous relief for the artist to know that the mediation of her work is in professional hands. It is also an opportunity to step back to an objective distance during the public discussion that is now beginning and she becomes free for a new phase of work. Every encounter with this species is a blessing for the artist after the lonely orbit in the studio and is a chance for her to see her own paintings anew through different eyes.

As Constant Gardeners are skilful at putting their impressions of the paintings into words, delighting in conversation not only with the painter in her studio or at her exhibition but also with her team and the visiting public, she also willingly gives her time to the texts needed for each exhibition – press articles, artist's exposé, catalogue essay. Once the exhibition is over, a Constant Gardener continues to champion the work within the framework of her institution, whether by bringing it to light for funding committees or prizes, or by recommending the artist for further projects. This is not done out of sympathy or friendship – although friendships can certainly develop – but because first and foremost she is convinced of the quality of the work and has no problem championing it.

The Constant Gardener also senses which of the paintings are suitable for the museum's collection and works to ensure that they are purchased and can become the property of the museum. With these acquisitions, the painter's works leave traces in the DNA of the museum and thus become part of its history – and of art history in general. The public will also be able to revisit the exhibition galleries in the online archive long after the exhibition has ended, just as the exhibition catalogue published by a good art publisher will carry the works further out into the world – and perhaps even turn up in the Tate's bookshops, between other publications on Kusama, Pollock and Rousseau.

All this means that the painter's work moves up in national and international estimation as arts listings and rankings are updated. Then – miracle of miracles! Suddenly the career *before* arriving in Switzerland *does* actually count after all, at least with Pro Helvetia, which sponsors the exhibition in acknowledgement of her earlier history outside of *la Suisse*. The penny drops even with the Swiss national ranking system Sikart, which like Trip Advisor rates the importance of artists with stars (1 star: local ground creeper; 5 stars: intergalactic celebrity). After a few hints from friendly advocates it finally awards the painter the three stars that allow her to supplement her profile with images of her works and a corresponding critical discourse.

Perhaps now one understands why a Constant Gardener can become an ally of the painter. Together they work to bring the paintings out into the world and make them visible there to an interested public.

How to recognise this species? Hospitality, joy, excitement, curiosity, discursiveness, the willingness to sit in silence in front of a painting and equal willingness to go out on a limb for an artist she believes in. You recognise them because they look at you openly and with interest in their eyes and when visiting the studio; they don't immediately dash off for the next train home. For them, you brew really good coffee.

Therefore: A glorious 21-paint-gun salute to all those Constant Gardeners who help the artist to bring her work to the world!

Classes of belonging

Now before we all get too comfortable basking in the afterglow of the Constant Gardeners, we should remember that the art world is also cut and thrust, a combat zone that is, metaphorically speaking, as red in tooth and claw as nature or politics.

Though it may seem a crude analogy, I enjoy likening the art guild to the hierarchical structure of the Hells Angels motorbike club and its classes of belonging. At the top reigns the all-powerful *Pres* – the President. Below the president come the Members, the associated art and blood brothers for whom everything is done and who in return do everything for the club. Next come the *Prospects,* the candidates who are waiting in the wings to be accepted into the club as fully fledged Members. *Prospects* have not only willingly subordinated themselves to the rules in force, but also imitate the behaviour of the Members to such an extent that they seem almost amorphous: the *Prospect* position is probably the most difficult, because one has to be faithful and compliant, but nevertheless do that in an individual way.

At the bottom of the pyramid, far below the prospects, are the Hang-Arounds, the useful human furniture tolerated as audience – naturally for their own edification – but not to be considered for any perks of the advanced entourage. The Hang-Arounds are often expected to do the unwanted and tiresome chores like lugging beer crates, working behind the bar, or organising the petty details of an event, but their practice as artist is rarely taken seriously; they come and they go.

And then, of course, there are those who, simply from the outset, ride the wrong brand of motorcycle and don't care about an MC insignia on the back of their leathers but prefer their waterproof Gore-Tex jacket with an integrated back protector to help them get around. Sometimes these cheeky cuties do a stint as a Hang-Around, but otherwise float free, with the penalty that they don't exist in the eyes of the *Pres* and the rest of the reigning entourage.

In art, as in life, the villain and his contradictions make for a good story. Therefore, we will now complete the bestiary of the Art-almighty with some of the less benevolent *beasties* whose path you may occasionally cross.

The Lip-Glosser

The English gerund allows for elegant and concise sentence construction whereas the German equivalent invariably sounds pretty clunky. On the other hand, the German language, with its playful use of substantives, can leave the English language standing.

It is this play of linking nouns together that first introduced me to the word *Lippenblütler* derived from the nouns *Lippen* ("lips") and *Blüten* ("blooms"), which is in actual fact, a botanical term, referring to the labiate species of plants like mint and thyme. I once heard it used, informally, to describe the type of person who gallantly and effusively vocalises support for someone whilst being insincere in their declaration – actually harbouring disdain for the person or work in question. The word is so onomatopoeic that I literally see a pair of soft rosy lips before my eyes giving rise to further rosebuds, which bloom with the slightest pucker of the mouth. Within the world of powerful Art

Deciders, there are those who would readily fall into the family of the *Lippenblütler* or what I will term in English, the "Lip-Glosser".

The Lip-Glosser is a charmer through and through. Friendliness, even courtesy, characterises his nature. In education, soigné, mild self-irony and the ability to chat amiably with everyone about everything, one is reminded of an aristocrat of the pre-modern era, so unquestioningly sure of their social superiority that they could casually mock themselves and their class in front of a bourgeois audience.

Lip-Glossers are always to be found at prestigious events in the art world, at openings in esteemed institutions, including their own of course. They are cheerfully engaged in conversation in small, private-looking groups of influential people, with collectors, art critics, cultural politicians, or their curator colleagues – and, of course, the Members.

If one overcomes the fear of approaching this illustrious art personage – or simply cannot avoid an encounter with them, the Lip-Glosser turns with a delighted expression, pronounces the name of the intruder aloud and then introduces her in turn to the eminent circle. This introduction is accompanied with glowing testimonials to the artistic endeavours of the troublemaker in their midst. It's then that you get to hear weapons-grade flattery like: "Frau Loomsden is an extremely successful painter!" Or, "It's amazing that we don't have her work in our collection yet!" (Compare and contrast that with the depressing news via your dealer, who, having recently approached the same personage about including your work in a group exhibition at the museum, was fobbed off with the put-down that figurative painting of *that ilk* is categorically excluded from the programme.)

However, the Lip-Glosser will now briefly enquire as to what you're currently busy with. The interest is quite genuine, for despite the courtliness, this art creature is above all a being of power and intelligence who wants to know what is going on among the artists within their domain. One might now think that the rule of the Lip-Glosser is secure and their dominion guaranteed, but since Art itself remains at its core an incomprehensibly diverse and shape-shifting being, the fear of something unexpectedly blossoming outside their circle of command is a persistent anxiety. If that were to happen, it would call into question his interpretation of the art to which both his institution and his life's work are devoted. So contact is also maintained with the lost souls who, by definition, do not belong to the illustrious inner circle of the favoured Members but who may find a welcome in art institutions elsewhere.

The Lip-Glosser then wants to know exactly what is in the offing. It can happen that an artist like the Little Painter, for example, barred from the Round Table in her home town suddenly receives a prestigious prize or large exhibition across the border in Germany, Austria, or France – or even, God forbid, in another canton of Switzerland, and now the judgement of the Lip-Glosser never to show this artist in their own institution suddenly looks askew. Has he overlooked something?

Though it might be galling to this type of Art Decider – embarrassing even – to have their view challenged by outside opinions and to see undesirable riff-raff climbing up the art ladder, the Lip-Glosser's natural instinct is to dig in further, close their eyes, stick their fingers in their ears and hum the little *Schlager* "not on my patch, sweetie".

Their exhibition programme and collection is of such long standing, honed and cultivated over decades, that it must endure as a legacy, even as the great, sweeping, shape-shifting art murmuration pushes for change.

You might laugh at this seemingly harmless diversionary tactic – but ignoring something to death can be a potent weapon. It is in this somewhat dim zone of appeasement, of satisfying the footpeople with the minimum of possible concessions, where the Lip-Glosser has a most important function. For lips bloom with effusive praise and appreciation for the Little Painter, who then, admittedly somewhat confused, again hopes to be able to make it to membership of the inner circle after all. Perhaps the museum will buy works if they are so astounded to find they have none, perhaps there will be an invitation to participate in an exhibition?

But no, this is not only a "fine words cost nothing" game, part of the social etiquette in the art establishment. It is a cleverly staged fizzle-out and flaring-off of system-critical energies. *Hope* in this sense becomes a form of entrapment, for those who have hope neither rock the boat nor turn away.

If the artist has something up her sleeve – an upcoming major exhibition abroad or a prestigious grant from the arts council that has been awarded, she can have a bit of fun by placing this in passing in the conversation to enjoy the gasping "where-who-when-how?" She keeps it vague, low-key and cautious, but for sure the Lip-Glosser is touched by uneasiness, fearing a possible breach to the fortress wall. She now chats coherently, intelligently about some art topic and then, despite the continued interest, withdraws politely from the conversation.

If the opportunity is at a good institution within the region or a next-door county, be aware, though, that the disclosure will be diluted in its effect as two competing emotions vie for the upper hand. Any disquiet at recognition for the artist from elsewhere is ameliorated by the fact that the chalice has passed, for the time being, to the neighbouring institution. At such times it is possible to read the typewriter ribbon scrolling behind the Lip-Glosser's eyes – "Oh thank God, that lets us off the hook for at least the next ten years!" Meanwhile, his lips bloom with the promise of drumming up support for the great event, activating connections with the press, galleries, the art public ... all empty words.

So when the Lip-Glosser effusively pumps your hand in congratulation for your forthcoming solo show in another well-standing institution in the region, assuring you that he will go all out on your behalf, then beware. Because then you really have to worry whether anyone will show up at all.

In difficult and lean times, when it seems the entire cosmos conspires against you, one can, of course, simply enjoy the sweeteners ministered by the Lip-Glosser, as shamelessly as when one sometimes has to scoff an entire family bar of nutty chocolate in one go for the sheer need of a sugar rush. As is the case with a sugar rush, the feel-good factor one gets from an encounter with a Lip-Glosser is intense but short-lived.

So take what is offered, enjoy the brief flash then put it all out of your mind. The Lip-Glosser will never be your ally.

The Secret Sippers

A further species of Art Decider warranting our close attention could be called the Secret Sipper.

In contrast to the Lip-Glosser, the Secret Sippers do really make an effort and actually come to the exhibition to which they have been personally invited. This speaks enormously in their favour because the Secret Sipper's attention is not exhausted in social blah blah but is really focused on the work.

Their most beneficial quality is their flammability. They can even be ignited by works of art that do not fit specifically into their defined field of expertise. The experience can put them into a kind of ecstasy of sensation, in which they become permeable, allowing the works to seep inside. They stand in front of individual paintings for a long time, look intensely, reverently drinking them in, take a step back, opening up the field of vision to neighbouring paintings left and right, focus again on the one in the middle. In other words, the Secret Sipper drinks from the work.

Because they are experts in the field, they will also comment on what they see, not so much in the sense of a classification of the position shown but on the personal encounter just experienced – because in fact this is someone who really knows about the core of the encounter between good art and viewer and the inner journey that it initiates. It is worth listening to them, because they speak from their depths and can illuminate aspects of the work that one has overlooked until now. In this state of perceptual ecstasy, their usually reserved caution is also suspended, and they express themselves freely and openly, so if accompanied by other experts, this can lead to long, stimulating and intense conversations directly in front of the paintings with peers as well as with the artist.

I have in mind an exhibition experience where the Little Painter was watching two Art Deciders of this species, both curators, who got into a kind of communal Pentecostal ecstasy in front of her large-format works. One could see the flames dancing above their heads as they stood before them, moving back and forth in front of the paintings, talking, pointing to the places they were currently illuminating in their fiery dialogue.

The Little Painter knows that her works are capable of igniting their viewers and that it is possible to travel with her paintings, to a hitherto unnamed, possibly undiscovered place within oneself. That is what good art does and this is the work of the paintings in the world outside the studio. Just as they can inflame the viewer, so too does the viewer inflame them. Ultimately it is the viewer who completes the painting by bringing her own associations and experience to them. Therefore the Little Painter does her utmost to enable them, not only by painting them but also by actively taking her work out into the world through exhibitions.

So when these two powerful Art Deciders are suddenly so set on fire by her paintings, it delights the Little Painter immensely, because it is an acknowledgment of the power of the work – and it could, *should,* mean that other exhibition possibilities open up for these paintings.

Afterwards on the train together, they chat about this and that, then when one or two of the paintings come up again in excited conversation and photos are examined on the iPhone of one of these igneous art beings, she has unexpectedly and surprisingly had a coherent and exhilarating encounter with two powerful Gate Keepers of the art scene.

In the following weeks, months – years! – there are hopes that something will arise from that encounter, something that could help bring the paintings further on their way in the world for additional encounters with other people – through the participation in a museum group exhibition, for example, under the auspices of one of those Art Deciders, whose upcoming exhibition themes clearly resonate with concerns evident in her own work.

In fact, at least two of the paintings that had previously glowed under the Whitsun fire are such plausible candidates for a particular exhibition that a whole year later and weeks after the opening – at which, of course, the paintings are not shown – a regular and knowledgeable museum visitor, who knew nothing of this background, enthusiastically declares how much her paintings X and Y would have fitted into that particular exhibition, even helping it out of a far too dry, conceptual corner.

Oh well, lesson learned. The Little Painter chalks it up to experience and turns her mind to other matters.

What an amusing coincidence it is that the German word for a tomcat, a *Kater* is also the same expression used to describe the throbbing headache arising from a heavy night out binge drinking. In the interesting case of the Secret Sipper who has displayed the traits of an alcoholic on a bender, the *Kater* is indeed as heavy and snarling as a Siberian Tiger. And so on the morning after the night before there is a promise to themselves and to the world never to touch another drop. God forbid that *such* paintings should ever infect their own exhibition programme and set off a chain reaction of ecstasies in their art public! Ashamed of their previous personal exuberance and articulation of the experience, the Secret Sipper turns away from the very works that have triggered this elation and given nourishment. The paintings have not only turned treacherously against her overnight but have also become infectious in their after-image, even dangerous to the daily bread of *art propre*.

The experience is dismissed as an excess to be forgiven. After all, it had been an interesting and pleasant afternoon, the Little Painter rather nice, if somewhat incomprehensible and apparently without a clue as to how much her work does *not* fit into the compartments, shelves and Compactus cabinets of the art establishment, poor bunny. Even if one actually trembled at the works – a curious effect, where on earth did that come from? Such indignity is definitely not desired for the serious art tracks of one's own institution, thank you very much!

And here the Secret Sipper takes refuge belatedly in the Three Monkeys Method: saw nothing, heard nothing, said nothing. For she was seduced and in a weak moment strayed from the right path when she spent an afternoon feasting on an exhibition that must never be served in the programme of her own museum.

That is why she no longer wants to know anything about the paintings that inflamed her, preferring to slide back into everyday normality, sitting down in her tin furniture, perusing through the many running metres of art catalogues shelved along the walls. There the revitalisation boost received elsewhere is discharged into the honourable art catacombs. The Secret Sipper upholds a system that not only does not generously pass on this work to the public but also wants to make it invisible.

How does the Little Painter best deal with the Secret Sipper? Loosely in the words of Dante: "Let go all hope." After Pentecostal excesses they will diffuse back into their Hades realm soon enough, to be neither seen nor heard of until their three-yearly drunkenness once again flushes them into an exhibition where they bashfully grab more interim provisions for their thorny path. Because their penetration into the work is, in actual fact, deep, their ecstasy before it quite genuine, the Little Painter can easily find herself again in the chamber of hope. My advice? Don't wait there for hell to freeze over but learn the lesson quickly: Secret Sippers, sadly, do not become allies.

The Tired Counts

A fourth species one may often encounter does not reside exclusively in the art world but can be found as a good-natured segregation of the patriarchy in all areas of society. We are talking about the Tired Count.

These art personages are also powerful art people, often presiding over medium-sized art institutions on the outskirts of an art metropolis. Their museums are the step between the small and the really big or important institutions; the rooms are usually spectacular and attractive for large solo exhibitions. Whoever can successfully play them also has what it takes to grace the galleries of larger institutions.

An overture from a Tired Count can therefore be interesting. An exhibition in their galleries brings the Little Painter within sight of the big steamships in the main harbour next door. But the offer has its price. The Tired Count is just that – *tired*, and perhaps a little bored of the rigmarole involved in bringing art to the public. This could mean that the artist has to do rather a lot more for the exhibition than one would expect, including perhaps organising much of the funding, or consulting with the graphic designer, or writing texts to accompany the exhibition. She can generally fall back on an experienced house team, because His Weariness is good at delegating to capable people, who all roll their eyes when it comes to his persistent non-presence, but who do their work expeditiously and professionally, more so without him, and are thus a great help to all concerned.

When, at the well-attended opening, the Tired Count awakens and gives a witty speech, presents the catalogue and declares the exhibition, including an aperitif, open and everyone applauds, the Little Painter's work is far from over. For now she has to drum up the press, bring in her own collectors – because the Count has become again what he already was before the opening: very tired.

She works like a dog but she also gets exactly what she wants, because *she* is the one doing it, and then doing it some more. The empty halls of the Tired Count's art castle can be filled according to the requirements of the Little Painter and her work, much to her delight – and his too. And really, it's not that different to what she's always had to do whilst trying to establish her career: namely everything.

To the outside world, it looks as if a decent if medium-status museum has finally taken her on – but she pays a price in this exchange of creative energy for prestige. There is a neutral to good-natured vacuum in the realm of this weary one, which she fills with her drive for the benefit of her paintings. Without an active host to engage with her work like the Constant Gardeners, however, she sometimes feels as if she is adrift in the embryonic fluid of her own echo chamber.

What advice about Tired Counts and their castles? If one has the stamina, then go ahead and occasionally get involved; but make sure that you reserve a sizeable part of your energy for making connections during and after the exhibition, preferably with a successful catalogue in the hand and by bringing in interested curators from other institutions, so that they see not only the works but also how you can deal convincingly with large museum spaces. And absolutely do make sure that you obtain high-quality exhibition views, which may require you to bring in your own photographer at your own expense. And after logging the show with the artist-ranking systems, spend at least two weeks on a Mediterranean beach or in an Alpine wellness spa, best booked before the exhibition comes to an end and the vacuum in Tired Count's castle sets in once more.

The Trojan Horse

Last in line for our little field study of Art Deciders is a deceitful creature – the professional, remunerated, institutional curator who harbours in his or her secret innermost being, a burning ambition to make a career as an artist. We will call this species the Trojan Horse, and as it is a rare and little-studied creature, the description of habits and habitat can be condensed into a mere short paragraph or two.

A Trojan Horse is not easy to spot until you are very close to it, usually you are seated and in the middle of a conversation/interview about your current exhibition. And because the curator-ally, your Constant Gardener, with whom you are currently working, has also been most specifically and especially invited to the meeting by the Trojan Horse, there is much to talk about and the conversation is animated. Initially the Trojan Horse will adapt to the situation, talk about your work and raise the possibility of a collaboration in the indefinite future. But when it comes to the crunch, it turns out that the next seven years are sadly and most regrettably already booked out. You might then want to prick up your ears for any telltale rumblings from within and perhaps also sneak a peek under the table. For the Trojan Horse is far more interested in passing on his own art dossier to your competent and well-standing curator-companion, and the professed interest in *your* own work turns out to be a ruse to snag a studio visit with the powerful and super-sexy Helen of Troy. The situation is embarrassing for all concerned, the chances of a professional collaboration in any shape or form is quickly reduced to rubble the instant the Trojan Horse neighs his true intent. Not only has his whinny violated the professional code of conduct, there is a reason why the Trojan Horse is not already trotting in the artists' herd.

With such experiences it's better to roll with it and then politely draw a veil over the whole thing, occasionally click the like button of the Trojan Horse's social media profile when it sends you its propaganda, for those who know how to use this situation to their advantage and groom the Trojan Horse's flanks may also find him amenable to doing business.

A word of caution though: One should not confuse the Trojan Horse with the genre of the artist-curator, whose exploration in the fields of art making and art curating is openly declared – and which can be quite fruitful for all involved. There are many artists who take on the role of curator; however, only a few hold influential positions at important institutions.

Constant Gardener, Lip-Glosser, Secret Sipper, Tired Count, Trojan Horse. Without doubt there are many more art beasties waiting to be described and classified in the vast art jungle. Some will be benevolent, others poisonous, all of them interesting. Which ones have you encountered?

14 The term originally comes from the Gospel of John ch. 15 and was used by the author John le Carré as the title for his novel *The Constant Gardener*, New York: Scribner, 2001.

5

Everyday woman and hero man – Gender roles in the art industry

Imagine a painter, a man devoted to people and the pleasures of life, who by disposition and propensity could also be a fantastic painter, but is not. He, who in his everyday life has no trouble being both in tune with himself and in harmony with his surroundings and who reacts to them spontaneously and with humour, changes his identity when it comes to art: a lonely and tortured painter enters the scene who does not want to paint with his eyes and hands but with his brain as a creator from the visual void, squeezing the paint to a flawless iciness on the canvas, as if everything is under glass.

You know what enthusiasm, warmth and devotion to the moment he is capable of – so imagine the trepidation in front of his meticulously cool paintings in which the stuff of paint is never even allowed to twitch, let alone take on a life of its own. A domesticated pup on the concept-leash, it must always cower strictly to heel, and "concept" is allowed to straddle the neck of the paint and break it every time.

His paintings have a peculiar coherence when they appear as printed reproductions, as if they had now arrived in the form they were drawn to, as if they had never wanted to be paintings at all but printed reproductions in the first place.

What is stopping him from finally giving conceptual painting the swivel finger and throwing himself into his painting, the way he does with life? My answer: The heroic tale of the artist legend.

The hero's tale

In art history, we know about the historical interpretation of the male artist as *artisto divino*, as a godlike creator, who, thanks to his stupendous talent makes it from shepherd boy to artist prince and unites telluric forces with those of courtly high culture. In the Romantic period, this so-called artist legend transforms into the figure of the great loner and seeker, and in the pre-modern period it finally enters the realm of the tragic, in which the artist is torn apart by the tremendous tensions in the social body – and sacrifices himself. After the First World War, the artist becomes the founding father of styles and -isms; although no longer divine, he is a solitary, self-contained and monadic genius, and from his aesthetic rigour and lovable bad-boy persona, he bestows the rebirth of form and shamanistic meaning upon the art world.

All this is heroic. So much so, in fact, that one has to wonder why there isn't yet an art prize in which a cunning 007-like gadget – a spring-loaded paintbrush, for instance, hidden in the soles of a pair of Dr Martens – is awarded together with the cash and accolades.

The heroic artist's collective energy expresses itself in his life and work, through which he transforms as an individual. And with relentless effort he also becomes the salvation of the collective. The latter is always rich in dramatic tension, so ideally suited to the heroic tale in all forms, whether ironically fractured or foolishly patriarchal.

Even in failure, in addiction, in destruction, the male artist is still heroic – if not more so. Even when disappearing, when dissolving, he does not escape becoming legend: think Basquiat, think Cobain.

Female artists also end up silent and silenced, as alcoholics, as suicides, or on psychiatric wards – but rarely does their predicament enhance their reputation or fame. They just disappear from this world, with no bittersweet collective melancholy, no concerned or emotional obituaries for their hard-luck tale in the feature pages. They go, and then they are gone and erased from memory. Their struggles were more or less the same as their male counterparts – perhaps even more existential than those of the male artist hero – and they met them just as heroically. But sorry, wrong story format, darlin'; no added narrative value comes from failure in the life arc of women artists or their deaths.

With the male artist, on the other hand, the heroic saga ascribed to him seems to work as an exoskeleton that not just underpins and supports his career but keeps him on a straight path from cocky bad boy to shaman to "silverback". He does not suffer from the sexism of ageing; the dents in his heroic armour only reflect him in a new, even more admirable light. And when he dies, the world mourns the loss of a hero.

The so-called hero's journey has been established as a narrative for millennia and per se creates a basic current of attention to which his female counterpart has little if any access. Even if they come to attention, they can disappear again just as easily. There is no established groove for *her* trajectory, which certainly doesn't run on the same well-polished rails the hero-artist's does.

The three nuts for Cinderella

In contrast to the all-encompassing heroic saga, there are three nuts available for female artists in the course of their lives, though these are offered as potentials rather than guarantees. If the hazelnuts in Václav Vorlíček's fairy tale film each unfold into the precise garments required by Cinderella for the given fairytale moment, the three nuts in the life of a female artist stand for three possible roles in the art world – Debutant, Reliable Art-Caretaker and the Grand Old Dame, all hard to crack, all a bit mouldy, with an odd aftertaste and hard to stomach.[15]

Let's carefully pick up Nut Number One – the shooting star Debutant. The art world, like every consumer enterprise, is eternally hungry for new names and fresh positions: the young, nubile art woman between 20 and 35 can be shaped and sold as a discovery that becomes lucrative for galleries and art promoters.

The young artist enjoys her status as a shooting star, receives grants and artist residencies, gets to know the world and its art powers, building a network and a name for herself with collectors, critics and patrons. The term shooting star is broadly defined here, not only standing for the total super-acceleration from 0 to 8000 that shoots you into international art orbit and envelops you in eternal fame, but also embracing more modest flight altitudes and trajectories. In any case, the shooting-star career turbo helps the artist escape the obscurity and anonymity of the many dozens of art school graduates in small or remote regions within three to four years. She moves to one of the art capitals and there becomes a brand that can hold its own in art and business, even after the shooting star status has burned out. Towards the end of Nut Number One phase she has, perhaps, assembled her art cohort of devoted colleagues, museum and press people, etc., who will accompany her – or so she hopes – in the decades to come. For it is these art cohorts, which one could perhaps also call art families, that support, promote and mirror each other in the art world.

It is now time for the artist to crack Nut Number Two and step into the role of Reliable Art Caretaker. We are talking here about the long, unspectacular decades in the art field in which the sexism of ageing dulls the lustre of her work – despite the increasing strength and maturity that is clearly evident there. Should her art practice become too precarious, the Reliable Art Caretaker may go into teaching in the lean decades, though she will neither neglect nor lose her profile as an artist. She may no longer be a hyped brand, but she is still a recognised art position, regularly invited and taken note of, who, with an increasing number of catalogues and articles in the art press, also leaves something of a historical trail.

It is in the second nut phase that the artist has to play at being something like the Grand Old Duke of York of nursery-rhyme fame.[16] The artist lugs her work up the hill, largely under her own steam. Although at the top she may make a fantastic exhibition with the potential to punch through to the next level, she has to pack the works up again at the end and carry them down the hill below the fog line, back into the studio. No skyward gangways are lowered from the next level above, not even a rope ladder. In the studio, the Reliable Art Caretaker has already archived the short press clippings, now she gathers herself again and starts the next uphill march.

She seems to be perpetually on the verge of a breakthrough that never actually comes. On the contrary, she is increasingly aware of the expectation in the art world that she should slowly and gracefully bow out, retire and leave the field to the new generation. And since she has not managed to achieve consistent and lasting success of an enduring nature, she becomes increasingly aware of her dwindling possibilities.

What is success?

Success comes in all shapes and sizes: Sometimes it is the private and invisible developments in the studio, sometimes it shows itself publicly and is visible from afar.

Every exhibition, every press review, every related discourse, every sale, every invitation to a public art commission, every prize awarded, is an incidence of what can be termed a "stand-alone" success. Stand-alone successes are remarkable achievements. They may not flow swiftly and directly to other opportunities but each incidence tallies up, together with the others, to an incremental overall progress. The artist returns to work and then begins searching for the next opportunity. Opportunity does not knock, it must be hunted down, each future chance must be sought out and secured individually, sometimes with the help of advocates, sometimes without.

The second more impressive, more spectacular form of success is that of the rolling variety. Rolling success – sustained success – involves a watershed moment in the artist's career after which she is swept up and taken along in the current. It is the golden ticket and as such it is the mode of success of which most artists dream. For this kind of accomplishment the artist needs advantageously placed advocates. It may involve an important museum exhibition with subsequent national press reviews and high-end discourse, where the institution procures works for its collection. Desiring to bestow further value and regard on the works in the collection and ensure an expanding reputation for the artist, other events are brokered by the museum on behalf of the artist in partner institutions nationally and abroad. This is the strong current that takes the artist further, deeper, quicker into success at national and international level, opening up prestigious high-end commercial gallery partnerships as well as a debut on the auctions market where sometimes the price label becomes uncoupled from all reality. The fact that a museum takes on the artist and her work with dedication and consistency is critical for such a watershed to occur. According to art historian Bénédicte Savoy art institutions are *Aufwertungsmaschinen*[17] – value-adding machines – which increase the monetary worth of a work of art as well as lending an additional layer of meaning to it. Although Savoy speaks of this with especial reference to the restitution of stolen artworks, such as the Benin Bronzes, her statement is valid for all art shown in museums.

However, one can and should see success not only in terms of the individual artist but also in the context of belonging to groups. Historically, for example, the success of the "male artist" has far outstripped that of the grouping "female artist". Male artists have collectively been on the path of *rolling success* for a long, long time. The artist group "woman" has celebrated quite a few stand-alone successes recently, but these do not fall on the same fertile, pre-ploughed and tilled furrows onto which the male success lands and takes root. For this reason, the woman artist hardly succeeds in docking onto existing lines of tradition and establishing herself there in the long run. Consequently, her work is easily forgotten. Consequently, her work also easily falls into oblivion. This is a catch-22 of course, a vicious circle: her success does not last because there are no matrilineal lines of tradition in the art world. Therefore, the push forward that her success should give to the whole group goes nowhere – and a new matrilineal line of tradition cannot emerge.

In Vienna in the sixties, the critic Alfred Schmeller praised the "masculinity" of Maria Lassnig's work in the *Kurier* in the highest terms, summarising it as "a sort of painting that is actually very masculine in its naturalness", as though this would be the only form of creditable praise available.[18] It is important to understand that there was no other possibility for positive comparisons because the lines of tradition were all male.

In 2010, I had a similar experience during a group show with a curator who found himself fascinated by paintings that exuded masculine qualities for him, but to his great astonishment had been made by me. I once encountered a teacher who habitually asked students in groups, which invariably had more than 85 per cent female attendees, whether, when painting, they were male or female ...? Do we have a choice? Is this the only binary choice on offer? And if so, is the male painter better or more advantageously placed than the female painter?

The ungenerous dictum that anyone who hasn't made it as an artist by the age of thirty isn't good enough and deserves a shadowy existence on the fringes of the art world, fails to recognise a reality that can be observed time and again in Nut Number Two phase: That there are a large number of artists who create significant bodies of work that are rarely visible to a broad public. Though the work may occasionally be shown, it is quickly dismissed into obscurity again, because it takes more than occasional exhibiting to achieve sustained success in the art world. Due to their circumstances – be it the political and social framework of their society, be it the conscious refusal to play the career game, many artists simply don't come sufficiently to light. It is in this astonishingly widespread half-obscurity that positions often mature which have little to do with the rather fleeting fashions of the art market. Is it surprising that many of these unseen artists are women?

Grand Old Dame

Let us now sniff at Nut Number Three: the position of the Grand Old Dame (GOD). If you're still alive at eighty or so, the late glory of the GOD may possibly hove into view. So if one makes it onto this pedestal, a window of attention opens that is equal to that of the shooting star but with completely different connotations. The GOD is also elevated to the status of a mysterious idol – think of Louise Bourgeois or Maria Lassnig for example, who did not make it to the top despite their original and outstanding work during their phase of Reliable Art Caretaker. In old age, however, they fell prey to a veneration that perhaps has more to do with the need for this type of wise, old, somewhat witch-like grandmother than with their exemplary biographies and their equally exemplary work. (Yes, yes, I hear you yelling: Lassnig could have made it much earlier had she not been such a difficult character ... But when did being a difficult character stop a man's trajectory in its tracks?)

Nor should it be forgotten that the status of GOD is at least as attractive to galleries as that of the newly lit shooting star that has just burst onto the scene, albeit for entirely different reasons.

Nut Number One and Nut Number Three share the popular topos of discovery: an art scholar & an art publicist & a gallery owner *discover* an old woman artist who, outside the art establishment and over the course of three quarters of a century, has created a body of work of consistent quality, colossal scale and compelling originality. The works are presented in the context of a large exhibition and a thick catalogue is compiled, while in the background the gallery buys up the entire oeuvre at a price that guarantees the old woman the last years of her life without material hardship, but which will bring the gallery enormous profits because, as a monopolist, it can not only determine the market prices but also regulate the availability of the commodity. Art scholars and art publicists initiate further exhibitions, prizes are awarded for the GOD's lifetime achievement and she is now regularly encountered in the art press. All this helps the gallery to disseminate the work and makes it valuable to the art market and collectors – even if the GOD is still unlikely to make it into the top 5 per cent of the auction market's stellar realms.

If one looks at the whole thing critically, the late and belated recognition of the GOD's work benefits the hokey-cokey of the art market and guarantees the market profit not to the creator of the work but to her discoverers, because the GOD, who just made it before the gate closed, simply has only a short span of life left.

These, then, are the three very different phases in the career of a female artist: the early sexy years as a shooting star Debutant, the motley middle phase of the Reliable Art Caretaker and the Grand Old Lady.

Miss the first one of these phases, which is often the case, and you've got what is termed the Matthew effect, a phenomenon where opportunity begets opportunity – and, conversely, lack of it leads to greater lack. Thus, the gaps between the rungs on the career ladder become wider and wider, and it becomes increasingly difficult to reach the next one. Unfortunately, there can be no reset or restarting of the game.

The bubbly young woman is expected to be invigorating and to inject fresh energy into the art scene; a source of pure new art. The middle-aged woman, on the other hand, is no longer dreamed of, even if she has made a name for herself and is still occasionally called upon. The old woman is revered because she doesn't stand in anyone's way or snatch anything from them but, on the contrary, becomes *the* favourable opportunity for others; besides, she has already survived disregard and indifference.

Nuts Numbers One and Three are preferably passive phases, one is *discovered*, promoted and presented. As Nut Number Two, one performs housewifely duties in the art world while the skin begins to wrinkle. None of these phases in the life of a female artist is even remotely heroic – in contrast to the narrative of the artist-man, which, as explained above, is structured completely differently.

In February 2021, the *Journal of Cultural Economics* presented an analysis of gender trends in the art market with statistics collected between 2010 and 2017 (National Museum of Women in the Arts 2017).[19] The research finds that women's artworks are represented in only 3–5 per cent of major permanent exhibitions in the US and Europe. This fraction is also reflected in the proportion of works by women sold at auction worldwide: according to Artnet's sales data, it is less than 4 per cent.

The great and fast drive-through bazaar of the Auctions Market is dominated by entrepreneurial, male buyers who are drawn to similarly entrepreneurial male artists. Honestly now, what were the chances of that?

Though the number of postgraduate qualifications is split fairly evenly between women and men, commercial galleries favour the male artist to the tune of 70 per cent, while only 25 per cent of positions shown at art fairs are women artists[20] – which makes Ivan Wirth's declaration in

2013 that "Female artists are the bargain in today's markets" just as true almost a decade later.[21] In fact, compared to the Guerrilla Girls' conclusions in the eighties about sexism in the Western art world, things have only changed by microscopic degrees.[22]

The Hero's Tale meets the Three Nuts – Interference currents both bad and good

The good news is that there is, and always has been, an extraordinarily interesting and diverse life and work outside the heroic saga of the artist legend, even if it is less historically tangible and barely preserved in cultural memory. The bad news is that looking from within the heroic saga at works created outside its circle of influence is damaging because they can only be perceived as deficient or flawed.

The foreword of this book mentions a small example: I sent my new catalogue to the director-curator of a Swiss art museum whose programme suggested an affinity for painting – a rarity in Swiss art institutions – and invited him to visit my studio. He declined to visit, lamenting the lack of a *roter Faden* – the red thread of continuity in my work; something that, between the lines, was just a reason to reject the works without ever having seen them in the original. Several years later, shortly before his retirement, he finds his way to one of my solo exhibitions and stands in front of originals for the first time. He is not unmoved and says goodbye to the curator of the exhibition with the words "Fantastic painter! What a strong artist!" *Well, thanks for nothing, mate.*

Maria Lassnig's biography states that she greatly regretted the lack of appreciation for diversity in the work of women artists, because she too had been told that she had no continuum.[23] The perception of a lack of continuity is a typical trait of those viewing art works from within the stricture of the hero narrative. The assertion, for instance, that my paintings do not all look the same was certainly meant as a reproach in my case. But here one could equally reverse the scenario to lament the inability of the Art

Decider to recognise thematic fields and their interconnectedness, as well as a lack of understanding about from where the vitality of painting springs – which is the fact that every painting is its own universe adhering to its own intrinsic laws, even though it is quite able to co-exist within a wider body of work.

I have come to recognise the gaze from inside the hero narrative in obvious sentences like this by one of the best-known, most widely read, now deceased art critics of Britain:

"The art market is not sexist. The likes of Bridget Riley and Louise Bourgeois are of the second and third rank. There has never been a first-rank woman artist. ... Only men are capable of aesthetic greatness. ... Maybe it's something to do with bearing children."[24]

OK, I admit it, this was more than a decade ago and Brian Sewell, art critic for the London *Evening Standard*, *was* notorious for his polemical windbaggery designed to divert and entertain the strap-hugging London tube commuter. On this occasion though, his views were being aired in the *Independent*.

Would you like a few current *delicacies?*

"All artists, inventors, scientists, poets, virtuosos begin in solitude." – "The void is a place of creation." – "The artist does not work for the sake of fame or applause, but because he has to escape the abyss within himself." – "The creative process begins in eerie loneliness, in darkness, silence and distance."[25]

These quotes are all from Manfred Schneider's guest commentary "Zeit der Geister – Wie das Virus die Kunst erweckt" (Time of Spirits – How the Virus Awakens Art), published in the *Neue Zürcher Zeitung* on 9 April 2020.

Is that me? Solitude, void, abyss, eerie loneliness, darkness, silence?

My creative process begins at the kitchen table reading the newspaper, me with the *Guardian* on my laptop, my husband with his broadsheet *NZZ*. My gaze constantly wanders to the upside-down photos on the front page in his hands, because nothing sparks the curiosity of eye and brain more than an upside-down picture. Or the creative process can equally kick in when our crow Dora takes a bath in a plastic container, while I, as her accomplice, shower her with the watering can. Or when she hides a glass marble in the hay and arranges the stalks over the hiding place with careful movements of her beak. Or in the traffic jam on the M1 North at Ratcliffe-on-Soar, when a seeping light suddenly cuts a row of precipitous cooling towers out of the hazy horizon line. Or the sharply cast shadow falling like a blow across the corrugated yellow-gloss envelope of some industrial hangar in the flat lands of Aarau. Or the wind-drawn condensation plume from the red-and-white-striped funnel of the waste incineration plant which, illuminated from below, stands like a sculpture in the night.

My creative process begins in seeing, in noticing things, in perceiving objects and patterns in the world around us – and as for ghostly loneliness, darkness, silence and distance ... Actually, I should urgently go to the toilet for a pee now. And a cup of Earl Grey wouldn't be a bad thing either ... Are there any biscuits?

One recognises the workings of the heroic saga in the pathetic vocabulary and the equally pathetic construction of meaning, which has little to do with one's own experiences, but serves as an updated version of the hero-artist in corona times for the feature pages of the *NZZ*. A big fuss with a lot of tragic words smeared over simple realities. Corona and art? The possibility "in these days of human emptiness ... to return in a kind of creative early stage."[26] Really? Or more likely, just five and a half kilos in weight gain around the hips, periodical blues and staying up until one o'clock in the morning to book a slot from Tesco's online food delivery service for my computer-illiterate old Mum back in not so merry old England.

For the Little Painter, however, it is important to understand that the view of her work from within the hero-narrative is by no means harmless. Instead of seeing diversity and richness, only a lack of structure is perceived. Instead of artistic innovation and tenacity being recognised, the work instead is judged to be lacking consistent style. Instead of noticing the cosmopolitanism and accessibility, even *touchability* of the work, the absence of patrilineal genealogies and lines of tradition are duly noted and entered into the register of sins as a further offence ...

All this runs through my mind as I stroll through the Taeuber-Arp exhibition in the Kunstmuseum Basel in 2021, where one might ask why it has taken so long for the art world to come to appreciate the characteristics of the women artists of the Bauhaus. The exhibition, which will go on to London and then New York, stands as something of a corrective as Taeuber-Arp has not had her just desserts.

Despite the declaration of equality between the sexes in 1919 when Gropius's school opened and the fact that more women than men were enrolled, the celebrated names of Bauhaus are all male – a gender that Gropius himself termed as "the strong sex".[27] It was these "strong" ones who mostly got to wield the paintbrush and the carving tools and who later were in line for architectural training. And the women? Well, as representatives of the "fair sex" – Gropius's choice of words again, they "mostly got to do weaving".[28] Taeuber-Arp didn't let that stop her, of course. She studied textiles and sculpture but also painted, designed interiors and made furniture.

Looking at some of Taeuber-Arp's fine watercolours, I feel retrospectively pissed with Walter Gropius for relegating women artists of the Bauhaus to tapestry, and further seething then occurs on recalling the premise on which this was based: women only think and work in two dimensions and are totally unsuited for the demands of three-dimensional design.[29]

This claim seems to have become so universally accepted that if you vox-popped it, I'd bet you could fill YouTube with affidavits that women have no sense of direction and misjudge distances, with disastrous consequences if they drive big cars – even though the insurance statistics tell a very different story. I say this as a VW Crafter van and ex-Land Rover Defender 110 driver who has become inured to offers from males to park the bloody vehicle for me, whose jaws then drop as I complete a perfect reverse-parking manoeuvre.

But a gaze that sees only flaws also damages what is seen. Despite being well rooted in my own history and having enough self-confidence to have steered my course unwaveringly for thirty years, I was troubled by the accusation that the work lacked a common thread, because it had apparently been impossible for that curator's eye to see the strength, beauty and integrity of what I had to offer.

However, there is no point in beating your fists bloody at gates that will never open and it is anyway quite possible that this is a generational pattern, and that, with the slow steady retirement of an older peer group, a much more open-minded approach will enter the art establishment. So, as also mentioned in the foreword, I resolved at the time not to answer the fine fellow but to file the experience away in order to write something about it one day ...

There is a second form of damage that the heroic saga template can cause – but this time to the hero himself. Remember the painter-martyr mentioned at the beginning of this chapter? After the hero has survived his own transformation into a hero, he is and must remain more or less exactly the same, a reliable and dependable benchmark for the collective: in other words, he solidifies.

In the field of visual arts, this solidification is celebrated in the artistic signature: the work should be unmistakably recognisable as the work of artist XY. This can lead to an astonishing narrowing of the oeuvre as a whole, as if the whole arc of development had been halted at a single point and then collapsed, as if the work had been created under the same influences, circumstances and conditions in spite of these being always in flux.

The *real* thread is that the gaze of the art powers-that-be – the curators, the critics, the gallery owners, the auction houses, the collectors and the whole huge network– helps shape what is created in the studio, because an artist who is already successful cannot afford to jeopardise his or her success. Routines are helpful for around the kitchen, house and garden, but in art they are deadly, even if profitable.

And the Little Painter?

She knows that creating visibility for her work and herself is and will be a permanent and demanding part of her task. She works and paints in the studio and then she works and paints some more. She's maker, administrator, PR person and manager; she's designer, text writer and fundraiser. It is important to her, therefore, that her paintings not be overlooked, important to demand the equivalent visibility her art brethren receive and not be satisfied with the second row or annexed sideshow; to be aware how easily things can move sideways on her. Then she must parry back, however uncomfortable, even if everything seems to be accidental and a simple oversight. Does she like having to do that? *Not really,* but she has learned to do it routinely, calmly and as firmly as possible because she has understood: if you are denied visibility and history, your present and your future will be brief. No one will know you, no curator will invite you, no journalist will write about your work, no art historian will discuss your paintings, no collection will buy them, no funding committee will be happy about your application, no building commission will invite you to their *Kunst am Bau* competition, no jury will ask for your expertise ... and all this will only banish your work and you deeper into the fog of the unseen and unheard.

"So, nope," says the Little Painter, "my name on the exhibition poster is exactly the same size as that of the regional hero artist." "Nope," she says, "the exhibition view of my paintings hanging in the group museum show should also be included in the online image gallery on the museum website". "Nope," she says, "it is not the gallery owner's freemason brother who writes the text about me in the catalogue, but the art scholar of my choice."

Why is one so prickly? “Well,” she answers, “some eyeballs have to be rubbed blind until they can see.”

15 *Three Nuts for Cinderella* is a 1973 Czech fairy tale film based on Grimm’s fairy tale *Cinderella*; however, it additionally gives Cinderella three enchanted hazelnuts that, once cracked, transform into the appropriate clothing to fool, ensnare and marry the prince – hunting outfit, ball gown and wedding dress.

16 “Oh, the grand old Duke of York/He had ten thousand men/He marched them up to the top of the hill/And he marched them down again/And when they were up, they were up/And when they were down, they were down/And when they were only halfway up/They were neither up nor down.”

17 Interview with Bénédicte Savoy by Claudia Mäder, in *Neue Zürcher Zeitung*, 8 Dec. 2021.

18 “Eine Malerei, die in ihrer Natürlichkeit eigentlich sehr männlich ist.” Original quote by Alfred Schmeller, as quoted in Nathalie Lettner, *Maria Lassnig: Die Biografie*, Vienna: Brandstätter Verlag, 2017, p. 149. Lettner further comments on this statement with: “Das war das höchste Lob, das eine Künstlerin in den 1950er und 60er Jahren einfahren konnte: männlich zu malen.” (This was the highest praise a female artist could earn in the 1950s and 60s: masculine painting.)

19 See Fabian Y. R. P. Bocart, Marina Gertsberg and Rachel A. J. Pownall, “An Empirical Analysis of Price Differences for Male and Female Artists in the Global Art Market”, in *Journal of Cultural Economics*, 46, no. 3 (2022), pp. 543–565: doi.org/10.1007/s10824-020-09403-2.

20 Ibid.

21 Andrew Johnson, “‘There’s never been a great woman artist’”, in *The Independent*, 6 July 2008.

22 The Guerrilla Girls are an anonymous feminist collective founded in New York in 1985 to make sexism and racism visible and known in the art world through informative interventions. The activists, who appear in gorilla masks, are still active today. See www.guerillagirls.com.

23 See Lettner, *Maria Lassnig* (see n. 18), p. 61.

24 Original quote by Brian Sewell, as cited in Johnson, “There’s never been a great woman artist” (see n. 21).

25 Manfred Schneider, "Zeit der Geister – Wie das Virus die Kunst erweckt" (Time of Spirits – How the Virus Awakens Art), in *Neue Zürcher Zeitung*, 9 Apr. 2020.

26 Ibid. Original quotes in German: "Alle Künstler, Erfinder, Wissenschaftler, Dichter, Virtuosen beginnen in der Einsamkeit"; "Die Leere ist ein Schöpfungsort"; "Nicht des Ruhms oder des Beifalls willen wird der Künstler tätig, sondern weil er dem Abgrund seiner selbst entrinnen muss"; "Der schöpferische Vorgang beginnt in gespenstischer Einsamkeit, in Dunkel, Stille und Ferne"; "in diesen Tagen der Menschenleere ... in einer Art kreatives Frühstadium zurückzukehren."

27 See Jonathan Glancey, "Haus proud: The women of Bauhaus", in *The Guardian*, 7 Nov. 2009.

28 Ibid.

29 See ibid.

6

Everyone loves a hero's tale – Two interesting ways of getting lost

The heroic art saga is an important interface between the hero and his audience. It shows him as a fearless explorer and shamanistic messenger of a sublime higher power, as someone who, on behalf of his collective, expands the boundaries of perception and breaks through to a sense of oneness with life and its many forms, especially when he has had his experiences in the realm of heightened danger.

The artist hero returns from his story enriched, an alert traveller who, though lost and overtaken by an unexpected encounter, finds his way home again – to tell those at home about his adventure and rebirth in art.

Let us suppose that the artist hero has set out on an expedition to the sand dunes and saltpans of the oldest desert in the world, the Kalahari. After dinner in camp, the late afternoon light draws him out into the red glow of the dunes. Forgetting all warnings of sudden nightfall, he hikes for hours until the day indeed comes to an abrupt end and the last light disappears on the horizon. Kilometres away from the camp, he finds himself in dark wilderness. The hairs on the back of his neck stand on end, for he has no experience of the desert night nor of the animals that live in it. Any sound could be a dangerous predator. Cautiously he retraces his steps as much as he is able. As his eyes switch to night vision, he notices from the corner of his eye that something is also moving on the parallel ridge of the neighbouring dune, as slowly and carefully as he is – and in the same direction. The fear of all his earliest ancestors of being grabbed and torn apart by a predator in the night overtakes him, but our hero suppresses the panic. He continues under the now vast starry sky, which makes faintly visible the trail of his outward bound journey – as does the unknown desert animal thirty metres to his right. Thus he is accompanied by the stalking footpad of some unknown beast, matching him stride for stride all the way back to camp. When the campfire finally appears in front of him, he is immensely relieved. The animal also then veers away and the desert becomes quiet again.

With danger receding our hero feels blessed by the unexpected companion. The gift? To feel for a moment as our faraway ancestors did, draped in animal skins on the wild prairies and dunes of the planet. And although our hero realises that the unknown creature was probably "only" a gazelle, its companionship touches him to the core – and not only him but also those to whom he tells his story.

Our hero is used to an eager and curious audience when he gets home – after all, what book, what film, what newspaper, what video game is not full of the adventures of men. Who wouldn't want to accompany him on his journey, because we all long for primal experiences, whether they come first-, second- or even third-hand? Not only men, but also women, because women have been travelling with their heroes as stowaways since the dawn of literature.

But, would a woman telling the same story from the Kalahari or a similar one evoke the same wonder, the same yearning in her audience? Let's put it to the test.

In the early twenty-first century, our art heroine travels alone to a big city in the middle of China. After an excursion, she takes a taxi and shows the driver the Chinese business card of her hotel. The driver, who doesn't see well, has apparently misread the hotel's address and, after a lengthy odyssey, evidently has no idea what to do with his foreign passenger. Perhaps he fears the heavy hand of the Chinese police, who might accuse him of kidnapping. He panics, suddenly stops at the side of the road and turfs our heroine out of his taxi in the middle of nowhere.

The nowhere turns out to be the sprawling docks of a gigantic inland port on the Yangtze River, miles away from the city centre and hotel. With screeching tyres, the taxi and its driver make off, leaving our intrepid adventurer not only in unfamiliar territory but also sandwiched between a thoroughfare with heavy traffic and the Yangtze itself.

It is February and rather cold. She is glad of her padded coat but, holy mackerel, she still feels the bite of the damp cold right on the riverbank. Is she worried? Yes, she is. Not wanting to feel too much like a stranded alien on an unknown planet, she looks around for orientation and spots the toothpick silhouette of the Fortune Tower in the hazy distance – that will at least point her in the direction of the distant city centre. Then she looks at the expansive, tawny river, shrouded in mist and sooty particulates, and a chain of immense rusting iron tankers slung low in the water. All manner of small boats of various design bob back and forth between the giant ship vessels, from shore to ship and ship to shore. Such a wide, industrious panorama, dwarfed by the huge river.

The Yangtze is not only China's, but Asia's longest river, a mythical beast born in Tibet and flowing into the East China Sea after a journey of six thousand kilometres, crossing so many climatic zones and regions on its long journey that it changes its Chinese name at least six times between source and estuary mouth.

Here, in this city of twelve million inhabitants and still more than a thousand kilometres from its meeting with the sea, the Yangtze is already so wide that you can no longer see the far bank, at least not on this smoky and polluted afternoon. The beast smells of diesel and wet silt and something prehistoric that knocks at a very old part of the brain – and so do the docklands.

Our heroine, whose concern for her tricky situation fades more and more into the background the longer she sniffs this foreign yet strangely familiar harbour air, places her palms flat on the cracked concrete of the river wall and leans forward to get a better look at the oil-smeared pontoons and python-thick moorings underneath. While she looks and looks again, and starts to draw and notate and photograph, she filters out the constant roar of the trucks behind her.

She, born and raised on the banks of a smelly river in a shipbuilding harbour city, meets one of the big fluvial beasts of this planet and suddenly feels not only welcome but, in spite of her foreign origins, invited to participate; even more, she is chosen to receive some of the gifts the river carries in his belly. She accepts them without really knowing what these gifts are and why they are being handed out, while she presses the shutter-release button of her camera again and again, taking note of the tiny one-man fishing boats, weaving their way between the towering tankers like tiny insects between boulders. She realises that she has switched into recording mode and record she does in a trance that makes her forget time and stretches space. After a few hours, she is exhausted but happy and what had seemed impossible before now happens easily and naturally: she makes her way towards the hotel, tired but high-spirited. She manages to flag down another taxi, with a younger driver who can read better, and feels, finally back in her hotel room, that she has been gifted with an unexpected, deeply touching and mysterious exchange.

Back in Switzerland her encounter with the Yangtze gradually seeps into her painting. At the end of 2019, she explores the gift of the river in several paintings of large ships. In the months that follow, these paintings become her metaphor with which she seeks to capture the force of an event unlike anything that had ever happened before in her lifetime – a global pandemic. And the city that had been the host of her exchange with the Yangtze begins its rise to worldwide, if dubious, prominence: Wuhan.

Our heroine lives to tell her tale, but does she get an audience? It turns out that no one – really no one – wants to hear the story of how she gets stranded on the Yangtze River, on the contrary, her tale is met with head-shaking disbelief and the accusation of having acted negligently. No chance to pass on the sublime experience to attentive listeners at home, no deep and yearning amazement, no shared reliving of the encounter with the mythical being, if only we could gather under the magical mantle of *Her* story. Instead, she is reproached for putting herself in danger. Fear and gloomy foreboding do not contribute to increasing the narrative tension in this case but determine how she is judged as a narrator.

There is no established groove for the reception of her narrative except for overarching concern for our heroine's safety and virtue because women are, after all, first and foremost sisters, daughters, mothers.

So what on earth does she think she's doing? What business has she to be out there on her own anyway, wantonly putting herself in the way of danger, silly woman!

Unfortunately, that experience is commonplace – for women. Media research tells us that women's stories are less willingly received and that accounts of *their* endeavours are outnumbered at best one to four compared to the many heroic sagas we consume daily.[30] Unless of course she is the victim of a murder – in which case, coverage is copious, if salacious.

And so we must conclude that we need not worry about the unsung hero but about the heroine whose songs – as profound and moving as the hero's – our ears refuse to hear.

But that's not all. She, who also listened spellbound to the hero's story of desert and darkness from a second mouth, becomes a kind of murderess when she stabs the belly of the hero's story with the dagger of the unheard heroine, thus severing its archaic magic. With her question as to whether a woman's story would also be heard in this way, she deliberately wounds the story and its re-narrator, hero-by-proxy, though a good storyteller in his own right. The tear she has inflicted on the cherished narrative fabric is clear to everyone in the sudden silence. The narrator, wanting to protect from desecration the life-giving force between narrator, narrative and audience, angrily vows never to invite her to listen again.

Yes, she defiled it and broke the heroic story all to pieces – but it was worth it to understand just how *ex*clusive the all-inclusive magic show the heroic saga really is.

30 See Leah Rodriguez, "6 Unbelievable Facts About How Badly Women Are Represented in Media", 16 July 2021, www.globalcitizen.org.

7

Rachel wasn't happy – An everyday case study

It's a cool mid-morning in a Swiss town. The Little Painter stands in front of an industrial building with a solid step-ladder under her arm and a complete set of tools for hanging artwork. A group exhibition of figurative painting opens this weekend in the former yarn spinning mill, thirteen men & six women, an artist collaboration.

She thinks it may be a bit premature for the drill, Rawlplugs, spirit level, etc., because it's the first day of hanging, which is far more about lugging the works around with artist colleagues and placing them in ever changing constellations until the entire exhibition looks right. But the Little Painter wants to be ready, *just in case*, because although there is a curator, there is no professional team of technicians, and you might have to drill a few holes.

When she enters the main hall of the exhibition, to her astonishment, the works have already been placed, many pictures have already been hung, all the prime sites are already occupied. It turns out that the curator and some of the art brothers had already come last night, set up the exhibition and distributed the works in the various rooms. The Little Painter walks the entire length of the space, round the back and down the other side to find her two big paintings beached in a dark corner, with poor natural light and no supporting artificial light.

Oh dear, she thinks to herself and sets down her tools on the floor in the main hall. Nine men are prominently placed here, but only two women – and one of them in a back bay.

Oh dear, oh dear, she thinks again when the curator resolutely tells her that the last word on the hanging has already been spoken. There is no room for change, the final decision has been made whether it suits you or not, and no, there is no budget for lighting improvements.

It is only ten o'clock in the morning, but the world already feels very old.

So the Little Painter takes five minutes out to think and to look again at where her paintings are standing. A bay with poor natural light, no supporting strips on the ceiling, an evening preview. She pulls herself together and tells the curator and the group as calmly as possible that she is not happy that her works cannot contribute positively to the exhibition because of the bad lighting situation and, conversely, that they receive very little from the exhibition situation in return. She justifies this with the long conversation she had had with the curator in her studio about the importance of good light for her paintings. A long, uncomfortable silence spreads. Then she is advised to wait until the evening when sunlight would flood "her" room – but could they please hang the rest of the work on the walls now? More evening light on the east side of the building, *really*? How novel.

Big Yachts and little dinghies

The uneasy feeling in her stomach warns her not to leave her paintings here because it would not only be a betrayal of her work but also cause acute pain. Although she remains calm and composed, she means every word she now carefully utters: she will watch the light throughout the day, but if it does not improve, she will drive up in her van and take her paintings out of the exhibition. They understand immediately that she is serious. Her statement triggers open mouths all around. – It is two art sisters, standing all agog, who are the first to respond: "Ah, come on, we're all in the same boat here. Someone has to occupy the badly lit spaces and think of your colleague X – she has an even worse space than you and your paintings don't look half so bad there!"

No, we're not all in the same boat, sweetheart, there's a big gentlemen's yacht out here at the front and a little girls' dingy in tow at the back. Although the Little Painter is feeling rather down, she explains with a coherence that surprises herself that she is first and foremost responsible for the visibility of her own work. This is the moment when the art brothers exchange glances, shrug their shoulders and nod. They suggest a long, brightly lit wall in the main hall, promptly carry her paintings there and swap them with a series of small-format paintings struggling to hold the huge expanse of white wall in spite of their male provenance. Once decided, everything goes with the greatest of ease and the hanging of the exhibition begins.

The Little Painter is the only one who has brought her own set of tools; the spirit level (one of the longest in the world), the ladder, the measuring tape and the extension cable prove very useful for everyone on site.

While she's busy hanging her own work, she overhears the curator telling one of the absent night-shift art brothers on the phone: "Rachel wasn't happy."

And why should she be? Has she been included in the decision-making? Or even been informed? Was it easy for her to speak up? No, no and no. The whole thing is an enormous effort of abstraction for her. The art brothers are all nice guys. You could have a beer and chew the fat with any of them – but together, it's as if there would be some kind of electromagnetic, chemical reaction linking them up to form a big cohesive super-molecule, where there is an automatic, unproblematic flow in how they organise themselves, naturally and unquestioningly taking centre stage as their rightful habitat.

And every art sister finds herself just as automatically, if not easily, moved sideways to the margins.

This is the moment when she has to abstract to understand that this is the habitat of a species to which she will never belong as a female artist. If a woman wants to place her own work within the fabric of the exhibition, she must first break the social code and the peace of the established art brother territory by demanding a redistribution of the walls, so that she can create her own sustainable environment within the larger field.

Naturally, this can raise hackles. And she is confronted with being difficult, behaving like a selfish diva just because she has disturbed the harmony of the gentlemen's club. The art sisters, too, who dutifully endure their role as social interconnectors, the WD40 grease for the smooth functioning of the whole operation, reproach her: she is endangering the cohesion because she did not back down and resign herself to the assigned place. Though later, over lunch, one art sister after another laments to her their own lack of assertiveness and announce they approve of hers after all.

Because all of this takes place in such a natural *fluidium*, because everyone is so innocent – the ratio of thirteen men to six women in the exhibition merely coincidental, the prominent visibility of the men and sidelining of the women guaranteed to be unintentional – and yes, because everyone is so, so nice at heart, it is difficult to open one's mouth and speak up against it all.

Of course, this is just another tool from the bag of tricks used to maintain the status quo. Not for the first time, the Little Painter thinks about the fact that the polite little girl in her has no place in the art world: so, either pack up or be packed away. Either she gets her work the place where it can shine (and in the process alienates herself from all her colleagues and gets a reputation as a difficult bitch – a warning label that will be passed from curator to curator) or she must accept that her work lands in a shadowy sideshow, though her reputation as an easy-going team player, greasing the social wheels remains *virgo intacta*.

How often does the art brother face this unenviable choice? Rather, he will rebel and puff himself up, everyone will smile indulgently and nod and think, ah, look, *that lovable bad boy*.

The French Moroccan author Leïla Slimani expands on the role clash between social interconnector and successful art woman in an interview with the *NZZ*.[31] She cites a recent experiment in Berlin with children between the ages of seven and ten, who were asked to eat yoghurt while smiling in front of a film camera for a television commercial. Two-thirds of the girls did just that: they ate with delicate spoonfuls and smiled prettily. All the boys, on the other hand, immediately spat out the yoghurt without any fuss – it was laced with salt. Slimani goes on to discuss the clash in her own life between successful writer and the inner "angel" as a stealth-trained social interconnector.

Later the Little Painter reflects that in one way all the artists in the exhibition, male and female, are indeed all in the same boat when it comes to figurative painting in Switzerland. All the artists should automatically be allies – unfortunately, no. From the very beginning there is a subcutaneous two-tier system and it's only when one or two of the art brothers are also suddenly forced to think how it might look from the outside that space is speedily made available and the position starts to shift.

It is like the cameras that Amnesty International sets up in the courtrooms of autocratic states: under external observation the verdict, already decided before the trial, can change and become more lenient.

The chilly morning in a former industrial building in a Swiss town did not pass off painlessly, but the sentencing of the Little Painter in this case wasn't so damning after all. It seems that she did not blot her copybook with her colleagues on this occasion. To her astonishment, they thank her for her initiative and acknowledge that the whole exhibition looks much better thanks to her intervention. Then, in private conversation and with lowered voices, the curator and two art brothers admit that they had known from the beginning that there was something wrong with the first proposal for the hanging and that they now wish they had fixed it right away and on their own initiative. It's nice to hear that. But the lameness of the apology does not escape the Little Painter. She feels torn between relief at not being made a pariah and frustration that the art brothers pushed her almost to the brink instead of rectifying a situation they themselves knew was wrong. *Blinkin' marvellous.*

It could have turned out differently: only a short time later, when she is once again struggling to make her paintings visible in another group exhibition, she is asked by the irritated curator what difference it makes that her new works don't get a good place here, when she is already celebrating successes that others can only dream of? He lists three of her museum exhibitions that had taken place five years previously – and for which she had worked her proverbial bollocks off at the time. Would an art brother of similar stature hear such a thing? Unlikely.

But we are now living in the twenty-first century; surely something has changed? Then again, "Sofagate" is the recent news from Istanbul, and Ursula von der Leyen, one of the most powerful women in the western world, has only managed to croak "Ahemmm" as her grinning male underling bags the only seat available, and she's banished to the translator's sofa. She should have smacked the pair of them, *but* delicate political situation, better to keep her mouth shut, even if she is inwardly fuming at the humiliation.[32]

Will it change? Yes, of course ... Everything is in flux all the time and at many levels change has been long under way, spurred on by pressure groups. This means, for example, that contemporary art collections include more and more female positions embedding them in the art establishment's DNA to establish new lines of tradition.

And yet also, No ... There is as well frequent backsliding. Soon I will be wearing a hip, black-and-grey ribbon on my wrist with the words "Covid-19 Certificate Checked: Access on all days", my Art Basel tote bag swinging from my shoulder, *business as usual* at last. But in "Unlimited 2021", a specially curated section of the fair dedicated to large-scale installations described as presenting "a wide spectrum of art forms" where "our attention and lust for discussion is on the rise"only thirteen of the sixty-two artists are women.[33] *Business as usual*? Seems to be the case here, chaps and chapettes.

"So, move over, darling": Women's quota or trickle down?

Uh-oh, gird your loins, people, and grab a box of Kleenex: the one subject, which can only be grasped with ... thick ... brown ... paint.

Balance is not achieved by retrospectively embracing the neglected greats of female art history and rolling Artemisia Gentileschi out of the depot. Lines of tradition for women and their artistic achievements must be actively introduced and anchored in the here and now. Like the Covid-vaccine programme, everything has to happen more or less simultaneously if the effect is to be long-lasting – otherwise the sociological group "woman artist" will find itself permanently trapped in the vicious circle mentioned previously.

So yes, please *do* do a last-minute recce of the older generation of women artists before they pop their clogs and never get to see how much you venerate them in retrospect (and how much you earn from them). Please, by all means, take a good look around to see the brilliant work under hostile conditions you've overlooked. Please remember that *everything* they have achieved in the backwater that the art world has allowed them has been done without constant pats on the back, without interested accompanying commentary, without reverential recognition. By all means, give them at least a slice of historical space by bringing their work more prominently to light. Because only the inclusion of more women artists in collections embeds them in the genetic material of the art world and establishes new conventions.

Of course, it is important to make as much amends for the past as possible, but at the same time, and with urgency, do this: take the cushions off the art sofa and have a good rummage to see what's slipped down the back in the way of recently overlooked treasures. It is, above all, the reliable art caretakers who come to lie there, the artists of the unspectacular *Nut Number Two phase* who are only so elusive because your eyes pass over them so readily. And then don't just look, but grab it, lift it up and show it off!

To all art purveyors and influencers, gatekeepers and trailblazers on the art scene: before you plunge into the next round of re- and upcycling the already well-established brands of canonical art men – which will undoubtedly get you the next medal of valour on your chest – please have a good look around.

Like other systems of commodity circulation, large parts of the art industry have a tendency to regurgitate brands that have already been established and tested on audiences in echo chambers. In this way, the industry shores itself up and reaffirms itself – becoming in the process more *state of the ark* than *state of the art*.

And: Don't make it too easy for yourself when you try to create a balance. No *buy one – get one free* à la now we show a non-white female painter, so we are exculpated twice over. It is hugely important and urgent to deal with racial discrimination, just as it is an equally important and urgent step to deal with gender discrimination: both have their own right and must not be played off against each other.

While the former colonial powers in particular must now take a deep breath and then plunge into the foaming rapids of reassessing their history and present, there are still a multitude of gender issues that also await reworking.

So if you're really going for it, avoid half-baked models like the men's yacht with the dinghy for the girls in tow. Leave the *women-only* exhibition concept alone, as recently seen in the exhibition "Elles font l'Abstraction" at the

Centre Pompidou[34] – unless there are really good and convincing reasons for it. *Women only* is a cheap solution that allows you to say: “Phew, women’s issue done, scales are balanced, for the rest of the programme we can do what we want again.”

Women artists don’t want to seclude themselves in exclusive women’s clubs, they prefer to be shown in the overall context and don’t fear the comparison with the art brothers. On the contrary. It’s not about temporary free spaces, it’s a question of budging up, we want to sit with you, after all there’s enough space.

Most importantly, however, you must be aware of the insane persuasive power inherent in the male-centred structural norm, how enormously receptive people are to it in society, politics, culture and education, even to the groove of the artist-hero and his self-perpetuating myth.

This has all been in place for so long that even the much-anticipated influx of women into prominent curating and directorial jobs in art institutions has not paid the expected dividends regarding the widespread inclusion of women artists.[35] Globally, it seems that female and male curators alike gain more influence and greater career advantages by promoting the art brother and leaving the art sister to the side.

Maria Lassnig put it in a nutshell: “You can only talk about equality when mediocre female artists sell just as well as mediocre male artists.”[36] Which presumably means that they are exhibited and promoted just like their male colleagues.

In a 2008 interview, the author and sociologist Sarah Thornton noted that in order to increase the reputation and price of an artist’s work, it must be auctioned over and over again.[37] This is still not happening to a sufficient extent with the work of women artists.

There is a remarkable story about how the number of female musicians in orchestras in the USA has increased since auditions there are conducted in a gender-neutral way. In these *blind auditions* – auditions without the jury being able to see the female or male candidates – the women and men on the selection panel focus only on the quality of what can be heard. This measure immediately led to a jump of 30 per cent more women being accepted into orchestras. The number increased by another 5 per cent when applicants were asked to audition without shoes to eliminate the give-away click of heels as well.[38]

How do you achieve a 35 per cent increase in the visual arts? Well, for starters perhaps, if publicly funded institutions were to commit to a quota for women, the figures for the gallery sector and the auction market would also follow suit sooner rather than later. Which would be nothing but fair, because these institutions sail on the flow of public money – and tax revenues are, after all, gender-neutral.

Recently I went to the theatre to see Poulenc's 1950s telephonic mono-opera *La voix humaine* (The Human Voice). The only alcohol dispensed in the theatre foyer, where I usually have a glass of prosecco, was a squirt of disinfectant liquid into my hands. After the gong went, I sat behind an FFP2 mask in the auditorium, witness to the final, abysmal telephone conversation between the abandoned mistress on stage and her absent ex-lover – and I realised with a jolt that I represented one tenth of the entire audience, five of whom were women and five men. (The Covid rule in force at the time did not allow more.)

On this evening, I experienced the coming together of two polar opposites: on the one hand, the single character on stage – "No, no, darling, of course I'll be good and not take a taxi to your flat and make a scene in front of your friends!" – on the other, the audience, in which every shift of weight on the seats, every crossing and uncrossing of the legs, every discreet clearing of the throat, every rustle has amplified volume.

Later, palms burning as I clap for the fifty other theatre-goers who couldn't attend that evening, I am aware of just how enormously it matters not to be stuck in the old role of the complaining mistress, but to be present, awake, willing to speak and participate, willing to do something. Because yours – and my – human voice, *la notre voix humaine,* is important!

31 Flurin Clalüna, "'Frauen müssen ihren inneren Engel töten. Dieses kleine Mädchen, das lieb und nett ist und immer zuerst an die anderen denkt'" (Women have to kill their inner angel. This little girl who is sweet and kind and always thinks of others first), in *Neue Zürcher Zeitung*, 29 Nov. 2021.

32 See "Sofagate: EU chief Ursula von der Leyen blames sexism for Turkey chair snub", in *BBC News*, 26 Apr. 2021.

33 Rahul Kumar (STIR) speaks to Giovanni Carmine, curator of "Unlimited" at Art Basel 2021, 21 Sep. 2021. See www.stirworld.com.

34 See Heidi Ellison, "Women apart: Spotlight or Ghetto?" on the exhibition "Elles font l'Abstraction" (Women Do Abstraction) at the Centre Pompidou Paris, in *The Guardian*, 21 July 2021.

35 See Fabian Y. R. P. Bocart, Marina Gertsberg and Rachel A. J. Pownall, "An Empirical Analysis of Price Differences for Male and Female Artists in the Global Art Market", in *Journal of Cultural Economics,* 46, no. 3 (2022), pp. 543–565: doi.org/10.1007/s10824-020-09403-2.

36 "Von Gleichberechtigung kann man dann erst reden, wenn sich mittelmässige Künstlerinnen genauso gut verkaufen wie mittelmässige Künstler." Maria Lassnig, as quoted in Nathalie Lettner, *Maria Lassnig: Die Biografie,* Vienna: Brandstätter Verlag, 2017, p. 306.

37 See Andrew Johnson, "'There's never been a great woman artist'", in *The Independent,* 6 July 2008.

38 See Bocart, Gertsberg and Pownall, "An Empirical Analysis of Price Differences" (see n. 35).

8

To have a voice

Just woken up, still in bed. Louvre blind half open to sky and foliage, the little cinema behind the garden hedge is cut into horizontal strips. A construction crane swings its arm over the sequoia, with a sound like someone playing a soft flute. A crow flies through, honking.

I have an elated feeling in my solar plexus, an echo of my dream before awakening. In it, I walk down Spisergasse in the old town of St. Gallen with a friend. She is a curator and art historian who once gave me a stonkingly good laudation on the occasion of an award ceremony in Germany. We come to the church of St. Laurenzen, the Protestant parish church of the city of St. Gallen. In front of the church, couples are dancing to the song "Come On Eileen" in strange, jerky movements.

Now, there's something about that Dexys Midnight Runners' song that always awakens bubbling joy in me, even though, like the rest of the world, I don't have a blinkin' clue what the lyrics mean – apart from the fact that Eileen had better come on, and right now!

So not only do we join in the dance immediately, I can't help singing along to the song at the top of my voice.

Now the worst thing in the world would be to stop that song in mid-flow, but that's exactly what is happening, as if the jerk in charge of the sound system keeps taking the needle off the record, interrupting the song, the dancing and the singing along and turning it all in to a set of spasmodic still frames.

We don't need that now, so I just keep singing the song, regardless of the technical interruptions, indeed, I can't stop belting it out, as loudly and as clearly as possible, until everyone is stomping their feet to the beat and we tumble towards the end, finally independent of the stop and go and stop of the sound system.

Speaking up

On a warm autumn afternoon in 2014, I am standing in the large, freshly renovated conference room of the government building of a north-eastern Swiss canton. In front of me sits a jury that is to decide on this very afternoon which works of art should hang on the walls of the three differently sized conference rooms in this wing of the building in the future. The rooms are all next to each other on the ground floor of the restructured east wing, an unobtrusive and solid renovation, emphasising the restrained and orderly beauty of the classicist building from 1864.

The details of the interior design have not only already been determined, but also purchased, right down to the rust-red barista coffee machine on the sideboard behind me, which, already in use, exudes the wonderful smell of freshly ground coffee.

Four artists have been invited to submit proposals, which, according to the brief, *could* relate to the history of the canton. Three of the presentations have already been made, and I am the last to appear before the panel of architects, building administrators, politicians and art experts.

I decide not to come alone, but instead to bring a 1.7 × 2.1-metre painting with me to the conference room.

Emporium – the title of the painting – "works like a shop window through which you look out onto the street from the inside", I say as I peel away the bubble wrap around the canvas and place the work on two chairs so that everyone behind their conference tables can see the painting with its curious composition. I stand next to the canvas, holding it vertical and notice the attentive, even amused faces of the jury.

"This room here, the regional government's biggest conference space, gets an additional window onto the world beyond politics with *Emporium*... Placed here" (I indicate the wall behind the chunky barista machine), "the sideboard with its coffee machine and cups are already part of the painting, part of the world's everyday assorted bric-a-brac – a reminder of the community which this council serves."

The brief given by the jury strictly limits the size of works to the centimetre and stipulates a square format for this wall. *Emporium* has the right height, but is significantly wider than prescribed. I argue that the long sideboard visually lengthens the 4.3-metre-wide wall and that a square picture is therefore less likely to hold its own than the proposed landscape format.

The hypothesis is tested on the spot and with the help of a jury member I put the work behind the coffee machine on the sideboard. The jury members get up from behind their desks, move back and forth, squint their eyes. When everyone has taken a look at the situation, they agree with me that the wide format does indeed look good.

At the end of the presentation, to my surprise, I am asked to wait outside for half an hour. That is unusual – the other three submitting artists had left immediately after their presentations as per usual with *Kunst am Bau* presentations and juries on a tight schedule. I agree but have to call the van-hire where I'd rented the bus to transport the works to site, and explain that I would now be running rather late.

In the meantime the jury comes to the decision to buy my paintings – but asks to replace a work proposed for one of the smaller meeting rooms with a painting made during a residency within the region. I readily agree to the request and briefly talk of the *Dashboard Talisman* painting suggested by a jury member to replace a work that seemed too "sombre" for a smaller room, whereupon one of the members of the cultural commission quips with a smile: "Mrs Lumsden, you are so persuasive, I suspect that you could sell us anything!"

"Probably, yes," I say with a laugh, astounded, relieved, delighted and a little shocked myself by the way things had worked out.

Why is it that a British painter with a C-pass (I was not naturalised at the time) and German only as a second foreign language, can sell paintings to a Swiss art jury for the conference rooms of their cantonal government? Without a doubt, the jury was an open-minded and knowledgeable body, the sitting director-curator of the Cantonal Art Museum a connoisseur and lover of painting, additionally familiar with my work. An atmosphere of generosity had been felt in the large conference room: this was not a jury behaving as if it had to judge an offence, pass a sentence and impose a punishment. They had the expertise to see that the works I had presented them were sound and of good quality and additionally worked well within the context.

How had I prepared for this presentation? After receiving the invitation to propose works for this space I had looked closely and long at the building, the rooms, the style of the renovation, and for several weeks imagined in my mind's eye again and again the paintings that might best suit the space and context until it had "clicked", not only in the individual rooms, each with their respective works, but also as a group of works amongst themselves. I had discussed the proposal several times with confidants to eliminate possible blind spots in my concept, so I had done the legwork and gone the extra mile and therefore could trust my proposal and go into the presentation with a certain amount of confidence in spite of the nervous tension.

In presenting my proposal, I knew it was key to show the paintings themselves and not offer a model with a couple of postage stamps representing the work, even if that would be backed up with a larger printed reproduction. Painting is a total wrap-around package that can only be experienced by standing in front of the original, where pictorial imagery, the substance of paint and the sheer physicality of the format itself come to bear in three-dimensional space.

This had meant effort, coordination and the extra expense of hiring a van, but wow! Marching into that conference hall with a large canvas had had an immediate effect – you could tell by the surprise on most faces.

The language thing

And then there was the language thing. As a native English speaker with a half-good ear for standard German though a pitch-deaf ear for Swiss German, I have to be careful what I say and how I say it.

If you, dear reader, have made it this far, you have also understood that I have set out to break a proverbial lance for the figurative painter. Moreover, before it actually breaks, I have no problem poking the art scene in the butt with it. However, I have come to realise that I also owe something to the tricky, ambivalent position of painting here. Its questionable status has forced me, and still forces me (even if it has since regained more ground) to think and articulate context. This, in turn, means that I have to make more of an effort and leave my linguistic comfort zone so as not to languish in the whiny corner.

For the presentation described above, I formulated ideas and observations, first in English, then in German. Then I revised the text until it was clear and articulate – or better yet, clear, articulate, thoughtful and witty. I cut the text into paragraphs, stuck each paragraph on an index card, numbered them and memorised the whole thing long enough to be able to speak freely and respond to questions – in German.

If you present painting to juries or other audiences, you also play the role of the hostess. Ever been to an awkward dinner party where the host is too timid or too drunk or too self-absorbed to bring their guests into conversation with each other? Well, it's the same thing with a presentation: you can't just go mute and hope for the potato gratin à la Dauphinois to fill the void. Your job is like chipping at the flint to make enough sparks to light a flame and start a fire so people warm up and become involved. And it is a job. I am not a born speaker, nor do I like to perform in front of people, far from it. If it were up to me, I would prefer to remain invisible in the background and let others do the talking. But let's be honest: who wants to be stuck in the dead end of missed opportunities and the endless loop of bitter afterthoughts all the time?

The jury you stand in front of has money and kudos to give out, not counselling sessions. Nobody will speak up for you and your work if you don't do it yourself. So get your act together, Eileen, and start belting it out loud and clear.

There are different ways of speaking up though. Blabbermouths use words and high decibels to hide their works behind a rhetorical deluge. Mostly they know that their work does not withstand professional scrutiny and so employ a smokescreen-lingo in order to claim otherwise. Their speech is a sales pitch formed along the lines of the shady second-hand-car dealer and they try to give you the impression their work is the absolute pinnacle of the latest and most sensational trend in art.

Still, these types are familiar in every walk of life and many of these bloviators will find their way into politics, especially in the UK.

Are you experienced?

As an undergraduate art student at Nottingham Trent University and later a postgraduate student at the Royal Academy Schools in London, I had two kinds of tutors. Though both groups would talk about painting, you immediately would recognise those who really had been down the *rabbit hole*, piddling in the magic tunnel and gaining experience – and those who had not.

Those who did not know personally the act of painting spoke wittily and with clever words, but it was obvious that they had no idea about the deeper layers of rock strata beneath their feet, and what it was like to stumble upon an eerily beautiful shimmering mineral vein down there, following it deeper and deeper into the darkness. They were simply not qualified to help you on the sometimes difficult journey of painting – which is not to say that they could not make a few apt observations about the works and place them in a broader context.

The ones who had had experience, to use Jimi Hendrix's words, and knew the *rabbit hole,* immediately struck a chord in me because they spoke from their experience. The similes and metaphors they used to get to the nub of the encounter were both highly memorable and highly applicable, and often ignited a fire in me because I too recognised this territory, even though you can only see it in any given moment from the corner of your eye. Their pit reports were also intertwined with their personalities and so didn't claim objective truth, but were more individual accounts of what it was like for them, what problems they encountered, how they eventually managed to negotiate them and what the quintessential painting G-spot looked and felt like, last time they managed to track the elusive bugger down.

Igniting penguins

Generally, when I have to speak about my work, I ground it as much as possible in my own personal experience of the painting process and avoid dreary, alienating art-speak.

In December 2018, just as my solo exhibition *Return of the Huntress* was about to open in the Kunst(Zeug)Haus in Rapperswil, a large bank from Zurich, which sponsored the institution where my show was hanging, wanted to hold a symposium for their employees with *Apéro riche* in suitably ambient surroundings with my paintings as backdrop to whatever affairs they had to discuss.

It was duly required of me to address the hundred or so stiff bank cadres who were now sitting in a block on neat rows of chairs like penguins who had lost their way to the equator and were looking for the nearest ice floe back to the South Pole.

The obligation had annoyed me. What should I say to bankers who just wanted to have a tipple and were hoping for enough crusty bread rolls with roast beef and grated horseradish? Perhaps then bumbling later into one of the paintings and leaving greasy fingerprints behind them because who knows what happens to strange bank-folk when they decompress from oxygen starved offices in Zurich with *champagne brut* and perhaps even the odd line of coke?

Whatever. Anyway, I revved myself up for a performance that would make it clear to the block of seated suits that my work was more than wallpaper for their symposium, and let myself be gripped by the arbitration-fury that had surprisingly set in while I was writing the speech and was just as surprisingly fun. I hang up a few extra fairy lights just to be on the safe side:

"I come from a world of clay, coal, steam, iron and smoking chimneys. From a pre-Christian pagan nature that Christianity has never been able to completely drive away," I told them. "Painting where I come from is therefore never afraid of colour, nor of grime and streaks of dirt; on the contrary, it seeks it out, transforms it to painterly matter."

Those on the edge of the rectangular seating arrangement began to turn their chairs outwards, looking about the gallery and turning to the paintings for the first time having evidently become curious.

"I stand in that British tradition," I continued. "The paintings you can see hanging here carry on this practice – unafraid of colour, of material, of dirt, of strong imagery and wild stories, because painting lives and will continue to do so – because it gives every generation the images they need to immerse themselves in this steamy, wild world of ours.

You are sitting in the exhibition *Return of the Huntress* and she's back from the wild hunt through the woods with her images – to feed into your fibre-optic, derivative, compliance world. No fear. Never. At least not in daylight."

I could hardly keep a straight face as I said those last lines (especially in the light of the dreadful and ongoing Brexit fiasco) but shock horror, how the faces had changed. The closed professional masks were off and they smirked at me just as ironically and cheekily as I had approached them. They turned to the pictures, discussed in small groups, asked questions. I had stepped on their toes, now they waddled animatedly through the show. The penguins had obviously acclimatized and started to feel comfortable at the Equator.

Before I climbed into the Defender and drove on to Lucerne, because I would be teaching there the next morning, a couple of the bankers came over especially to see me off with a handshake.

On the nocturnal highway through Säuliamt, I thought how necessary it had been to rev the bankers up with words, so that the invisible barrier between them and the work could dissolve and disappear.[39] It had been no more than an honest if rather souped-up tale of soot and smoke and, admittedly, a few sideswipes at the disembodied world of money, but that had been enough for the gang to wake up and open their eyes. Well, probably the champers at the beginning had also helped. So much for speaking up.

Writing down

Then there is the writing down.

The life of an artist is generally not free of writing. There is always paperwork to be done, whether it's for grant applications, work reports, written interviews, contributions to press and media work, references and reports for art mentees, or texts about other artists' work when working as an artist-curator. You have to put things into written form whether you like it or not.

For a long time, funding applications in particular caused me trouble and torment because a project description or a "concept" always has to be a necessary part of the application. Well, my painting cannot be hemmed in by a concept. I want to paint, not invent an artistic framework for painting in order to be able to apply for a work grant. But what could be offered instead of a concept? It is clear that funding bodies have to have something in their files to legitimate the arts sponsorship they offer, coming as it does from the taxpayer's purse.

After years of trying and failing – or worse of trying, succeeding and then having to deliver on a project that was a misery of conceptual stricture, I finally decided I'd never do that again and instead would offer the smells, sights and sounds from down the rabbit hole or, in other words, my experiences and insights with, in and from the act of painting.

In this new approach there was no dance around the golden concept-calf, no fake brain-loops, no project yoga, no bullshit but just talking about the experience of painting, of visual perception and the trajectory of the work. I consciously refrain from using too much technical language, because I'm a painter, not an art historian.

Believe it or not, it has worked ever since – not that I'm making applications all the time, because having had the privilege of receiving some grants, I don't want to always be pushing my work under people's noses again for more – until there is a good and valid reason to do so.

I am still lying in bed, taking the last sip of my morning coffee. A second crow flutters through the garden, with a honk. That's okay, let them shout as loud as they want. Because I too can blare out my song into this world.

39 Säuliamt is the Affoltern district in the canton of Zurich.

9

Teaching and to be taught – The Ping-Pong of art education

"I'll never teach again for the rest of my life!" I promised Helene, my co-student, in autumn 1991 under the swoop of twittering starlings. We sat there on a grassy hill in Leicester's city centre where once had stood a Roman fortress, just a few years before the bones of Richard III, the last English king killed in battle, were discovered under a nearby parking lot in the Greyfriars Priory.

It was there that we were approaching the end of a one-year postgraduate course in Art Teaching at De Montfort University, after graduating with a Bachelor in Fine Art at Nottingham Trent University and a further year with an empty wallet and a studio without heating or running water. Teaching was Plan B and a sop to my mother, who had been nagging me forever and a day to get a real job.

I finished with a first-class grade to teach but instead went back to another five years in freezing studios in provincial cities, punctuated by occasional stints of part-time teaching in colleges or grimy jobs in homes for elderly people or packing sausages in meat factories or washing up in the kitchens of the local Freemasons lodge.

The foundation course with eighteen at Nottingham Polytechnic had been a blast. Not only had I found my peers but also Ken Lee, an unconventional and free-spirited tutor. Playwright, stage designer and painter, he loved figurative painting and encouraged our potential. Back then it was as though a whole new and unexpected world had opened up to me, a living world of art rather than something relegated to the history books. We would gather on the external causeways of high-rise social housing blocks, dodging pools of slowly evaporating urine, to draw and paint the grunge and routine of the inner city. Paint, I found, was the visceral, crusty material most suitable for the task.

Art school, I thought then, was my real home, and a BA in Fine Art would settle me there firmly. But the BA did not only mean specialisation, allowing the painter in me to emerge, it also broke up the Art Family of the foundation course into many little booths, where one would work alone, often rather lost under the principle of "Genius, teach thyself".

"The British can't paint"

Said one of my Nottingham tutors once. I have often thought back to the man who believed that the British lacked the basic, essential condition of light to such an extent as to curtail the development of painting. But then I've always thought that there is a lot to be said for British "murkiness" – a condition where it is unclear where one form begins and another comes to an end – and there precisely is to be found the zone of ambivalence where good painting really begins.

My BA, in fact, was quite similar to the following years out in the wild as an unknown painter on the dole who sometimes couldn't afford her cup of coffee at the all-night Greasy Spoon Cafe. These were odd and rather uncomfortable times, Bohemia nothing but a figment in a late nineteenth-century novel.

I worked on the fifth floor of an old red-brick Victorian factory, in an architectural blip protruding from the main flank of the building, housing not only my tiny room but also the access stair. There I excavated all the walls right back to the plaster, by gluing muslin onto them and ripping off the ancient layers of arsenic blue and distemper yellow paint, to work over these hangings to make my paintings.

In plan, the room was almost triangular, but with rounded corners, a bank of sashes on two sides, so that from the street, as I worked on late into the night, the light behind all the other windows extinguished, it looked rather like a lighthouse beacon with me as the moving wick inside it.

Like moths to a flame came the girl gangs of St. Ann's, trying to break my door in and threatening via the intercom to stab me. Nottingham then was a city known for its undercurrent of violence and vice, where one could be assaulted in telephone boxes in broad daylight or equally experience attempted grooming by pimps. There were occasions when I really had to leg it in order not to be beaten up, or worse. Nasty encounters were almost considered to be an occupational hazard for females living alone.

I lived in a little flat above a Scottish butcher's shop, where freezer trucks unloaded carcasses in the middle of the night, to be dismantled with the chopper somewhere underneath my mattress. The stench of blood and bone only dissipated when the night shift of the bakery next door took a cigarette break on the fire escape: then the smell of freshly baked bread briefly filled the courtyard. *Life was nocturnal.*

And the art scene in Nottingham was, as is often the case in provincial towns, a strange mix of tiny and closed-off fiefdoms and well-meant artists' initiatives that regularly petered out in the wasteland between our studios and exhibition opportunities of consequence.

If you wanted to move on from this sort of existence there was actually only one place to go: London, being not only the political, economic and media hub of the UK, but of the art world too.

The Royal Academy and HRT, darlings!

Here, there were indeed chances for a better life: the Royal Academy in London was not just a notable museum but housed the oldest art school in Britain, with J. M. W. Turner and John Constable belonging to the alumni. It offered – with its three-year postgraduate studies for painting (not in the Bologna system, but equivalent to an MA) – not only heated painting studios with cast-iron radiators on legs, as though they'd just walked in and made themselves comfortable, but a sizeable bursary that helped cover most of the high living costs in the British capital as well as part-time jobs in the "front of house" cloakroom or in the fund-raising department of the museum.

In the Vaults – the catacombs at the back of the prestigious museum at Burlington House, Piccadilly, where the "Schools" were accommodated, there was a quarter-mile of vaulted lamp-lit corridor, flagstones polished smooth with countless footfalls and lined with so many marble busts and statues as to be reminiscent somehow of the bleak palace of the white witch of Narnia, where many a hapless two- and four-legged creature had been turned to stone.[40] Here one traversed between contemporaneity and antiquity several times a day, between front-of-house hub with blockbusting exhibitions and the deeper vaults and secret spaces of our own studios.

To be accepted into the RA Schools, you submitted a portfolio. If you made it to the second round, you went before a panel of eight Royal Academicians who were to find out if you were worthy of stepping over the same flagstones as many notable artists had done before. Each year, fifteen painters and three sculptors would be chosen from hundreds of applicants; the Royal Academy Schools had no more than fifty-four students at any one time and was considered, side by side with the Royal College, the Slade and Goldsmiths, as the top end of art education in Britain.

I'd get off the tube at Green Park and walk along Piccadilly (in awed raptures when I first arrived) and then up through Burlington Arcade, past the livery guards and the boutiques, their bowed windows full of high-end goods. At the other end, where Burlington Gardens met Cork Street, I'd come out and make a sharp U-turn around the corner, walking the entire length of the arcade again, but this time on the reverse side, down a long back alley with soot-streaked walls so tall it was like passing through a ravine. This was the ramshackle, smutty backstage to the pomp and splendour of the *front-of-house museum* and all the bling of Piccadilly between Fortnum's and the Ritz. We had to sign in with the guard on the door, then, before heading to the studios, we stopped by the small student cafeteria on the mezzanine, grabbed a cup of tea and peered into the pots of Khalid, our lovely chef from Morocco, curious to know what would be on the table for lunch.

The year I was admitted, there was an unexpected change in the RA Schools, which had always been known not only for providing their students with a generous infrastructure of studios and workshops but also for giving them the enormous and much-appreciated freedom to determine their own course of development over three years, so much so that in the 1960s, for example, David Hockney, who was actually enrolled at the Royal College, could often be found working in the RA Schools, where he could obviously do more of his thing and no one minded. Leonard McComb, the new *Keeper* – the director/administrator – of the RA Schools, however, saw things quite differently.

Instead of letting us students develop our work naturally within a contemporary framework, he made a sudden backward inflection and tried to pack us off to the Life Room day in, day out – a half-moon amphitheatre with curved wooden benches like crooked church pews, overseen by the plaster-cast cadaver of some long-since executed criminal, peeled like a grape and arranged in death as a crucifixion, no doubt to service those artists commissioned to make a work on the Passion of Christ.

Here then, under Leonard's tutelage, we were not only to become anatomy experts but also to imitate his own swirly, mannered watercolour style – as with the ancient master-pupil rites of old.

Nothing against a bit of life drawing – it's in fact a good exercise for hand and eye – but it is quite enough to do it once or twice an evening in the week and besides I'd already done oodles of it on my BA. We were postgraduates not fledglings on a foundation course – for da Vinci's sake!

We had come here because we wanted to immerse ourselves in the art life of a cultural capital, not to feel Leonard's stale breath on the back of our necks while we stared at a bony arse! And not only that, the old geezer in his wire-framed glasses and pinstripe suit was telling me what brush to use and exactly where to put it on the paper. I knew precisely where I wanted to stick my brush ...

Meanwhile, the front-of-house Museum was showing *Sensation!* – the hippest, most contemporary show ever seen, with works from the Saatchi collection and all the Brit-pack artists represented, for which people were queuing twice around the block to get a ticket.

Leonard's return to the antiquities sparked a rebellion in the student body, and some of us began organising the Red Square Lectures, a series of guest lectures by well-known artists to compensate for all the contemporary guest tutors Leonard deprived us of.[41] But these weren't small informal events in the Schools – they were huge events in the *Front of House*, within the Reynolds room of the museum. Red Square brought people like Dinos & Jake Chapman or John Stezaker to the RA for debates on topics like "Monstrosity and Sexuality in Contemporary Art" (1997).

When I was back in London this year – 2022 – going through my archive, I found the posters for these events, with the RA crest at the top and our names as the organisers at the bottom.

I remembered then perching on the corner of Norman Rosenthal's desk as he handed me the phone so that I could explain our plan to George and invite him and Gilbert to participate.[42] That phone call then had us running off to Cork Street behind the RA – then the centre of the gallery district – where we negotiated with gallerist Victoria Miro, who helped us engage Dinos & Jake that same afternoon. The fact that Gilbert and George declined to participate on this occasion didn't seem to matter. The RA "Secretary" (Director) David Gordon, gave us a small budget to take the Chapman brothers and John Stezaker to lunch at Quo Vadis in Soho, as well as other possible candidates for Red Square – Matthew Collins, Sarah Kent, Richard Patterson, Ian McKeever, Emma Dexter and Peter Doig ... to name but a few. Tracey Emin, however, dispatched my fellow student Gerwyn with a brusque "Fawk orf!" So we missed her, as another much needed female voice.

These debates, held in the Reynolds room of the RA, were packed out with art students, critics and curators, piling in from all over London so that there weren't even enough seats for everyone to sit down. The third event was curtailed by the great RA fire in 1997, where the evening ended in a vast evacuation not just of people but of manuscripts and works of art, carried out to safety by the London fire brigade, while the fire itself burnt upwards through the temporary roof over one of the galleries rather than spreading sideways.[43] I remember that it was Sherwyn Mason, one of the guards, who saved the night by taking the so-called "glitch" in the fire alarm system seriously enough to investigate and get us all out.

In the day we painted in our top-lit studios in overalls and clogs and would occasionally nip out to an arcade off Bond Street to buy chocolate, always in our ripped and paint-splattered togs. There seemed, on the surface at least, to be something amazingly egalitarian about it all, the doors of Gucci and Tiffany's would be opened for us and we'd be invited in, because nobody knew who had a fat wallet in their back pocket and the rich were just as likely to have ripped and splattered clothes as we did.

On winter evenings I would go to Tate Britain in Pimlico or the Hayward Gallery, getting off the Tube at Charing Cross and traversing the Thames via the pedestrian walkway attached to the side of the railway bridge with Arvo Pärt's *Fratres* or Gesualdo's *Lamentations* in my ears, music introduced to me by John Stezacker. If, on top of that, snowflakes swirled through the darkness of the city at night – which sometimes happened even in London – I was in heaven.

At the private launch parties of new exhibitions at the RA, I was often employed to act as a chaperone for journalists or photographers so that the press didn't accost, say, Jarvis Cocker or Salman Rushdie – cautiously mingling under threat of the fatwa – or Kylie Minogue weaving between Hirst's flock of sheep in formaldehyde, without first being asked by the chaperone. I would also sell raffle tickets at the summer ball, a spectacular romp with extravagant food and drink, light shows and secret bars among the art installations. A candy wagon on wheels with an awning striped like peppermint rock always stood at the top of the main staircase with all the jelly beans and sherbet lemons one associates with a Victorian childhood and advanced tooth decay. It all smelt of champagne and by the end of the night one would perhaps see Nick Cave slouched, the worse for wear, at the foot of the paintbrush-wielding statue of Reynolds, or Jibby Bean, former Vivian Westwood model of the sixties, art dealer and club hostess (who also was a guest speaker in our Red Square events) wobbling on stilettos, young guy on her arm, calling to us over her shoulder: "HRT, darlings, HRT!"[44]

We students had the chance to show our work in the annual "Premiums" exhibition in the RA galleries, shoulder to shoulder with modernist artists like Braque or Giacometti, the two names on the programme when *our* "Premiums" took place. It brought our work to larger, also international audiences. One then met people from Switzerland, for example – and I discovered afterwards that one Gentleman had even bought a work, thus beginning a long, steadfast friendship.

(A word of caution though: you may find yourself travelling as a result of such connections. In that event, beware of paragliding. You may find yourself first crash-landing on

Graubünden's Mount Corvatsch with a broken back and later in a rehabilitation centre, where the doctors are rather hot, if perplexing.)

The deceitful bones of Richard III and angels with pencils

Teaching was indeed no longer an issue for me after the RA, until a few years later when the *Fremdenpolizei* (The Foreign Police) of St. Gallen came knocking, concerned about the poor state of my bank account in conjunction with the separation papers pertaining to my failed marriage. The rather pragmatic and not especially unsympathetic interview quickly boiled down to this: "Start earning regular money, otherwise back to merrie olde England, Frau Loomsden."

Of course, this encounter was nothing in comparison to the current points system for migrants in Britain in 2021, where foreigners are viewed as dud entities of economic encumbrance whose laden little dinghies bob up and down on the wintry waves of the English Channel.

Anyway, that was the start of a chain of teaching posts, which culminated eventually in a blind application to the vice director and head of art at a university in Central Switzerland, a German who appreciated figurative painting. And so began a twelve-year stint of teaching. I was thrilled to get a small, part-time post on the Foundation course at first and then some hours on the undergraduate BA course for Fine Art, where for a short time at least I was "keeping the seat warm" for the administrative head of department, who at some unspecified time in the future anticipated wanting to leave admin and return to the classroom.

By the time the bones of Richard III the Plantagenet King of England were unearthed under the car park back in Leicester in 2012, I had been breaking the promise I made to Helene there for several years: I was teaching as a tenured art lecturer at the university on the campus known as the "Sentimatt".

The Sentimatt was a converted factory where the Schindler company had once manufactured lifts, situated on a strip of alluvial land between the left bank of the Reuss and the turreted Chateau Gütsch, where old Queen Victoria had liked to holiday. The location fell outside the boundaries of the pretty old town, which by being additionally surrounded by lake and mountains made it a honey-trap for tourists, and therefore constantly overrun.

The river Reuss flows parallel to the Sentimatt, sometimes so swollen by high water that its level rises almost to the top of the graffiti-covered concrete retaining wall. Both motorway and railway intersect the river at this point, so you always had a great sense of flow in the Sentimatt. This was good, not just for art students but for all the ghosts of the past too, all the poor souls who'd been executed on the no man's land where the railway bridge now stood and the nearby Totenacher, where their corpses, along with those of prostitutes and suicides, were buried. On the other side of the tracks is Baselstrasse, the place where Lucerne comes closest to having inner city buzz.

And there on the bachelor course for art, I was inundated with requests for tutorials from students clamouring for guidance on how to approach painting. This happened not only in the painting module I was brought in to develop, but also in other, more general modules in which I participated as a lecturer throughout the semester.

I enjoyed teaching mainly because of the students. I was amazed by the free-flowing exchange between the sexes, because with art students there is less of a gender-divide and more of a gender-join. Not in the sense that everyone is coupling up – though that too of course – but more because of the real friendships between the sexes, without needing a sexual relationship as a basis per se. In any case, the distinction between the sexes was toned down and softened, which created mutual understanding and common ground, something I had missed in my own student years.

Most of the time I came home from teaching full of hope, hope for these young people and for what they would bring with them into the world. This is also the reason why as a lecturer I often had the impression that my main task was to raise a kind of invisible dome under which the students would find both the space and the place for their unforeseeable developments. Because art education is not linear, but lateral. It is the lateral processes that make it possible to create new pathways in the brain and in creative routines.

Parallel to the wonder of the students, however, I had also discovered that Central Switzerland was influenced by a somewhat unique conception of art known as "Innerschweizer Innerlichkeit" (ISI) roughly to be translated as "Inner-Swiss inwardness". Those who professed this aesthetic orientation behaved like depressed angels with Caran d'Ache pencils: every stroke is sacred – many of them invisible. Painting? Much too loud. Much too big. Much too colourful. You take "Bildli" with a Polaroid and make figurative painting in a hobby course at the Migros Klubschule.[45] For the Central Swiss Art Hermit, art had to be sensitive and translucent, dignified and perfect. The fact that this kind of highly aesthetic work never ever offends anyone's feelings probably doesn't require further explanation.

ISI did not prevail everywhere: the Fumetto comic festival was always bright, loud, exciting and international; the art museum similarly outward looking and international, the music scene famously so. Nor was it evident in the design department.

I've no idea who succeeded in intimidating part of the Central Swiss artistic community to such an extent that it turned into an ascetic order of silence – perhaps a haunting by patron saint and abstemious hermit Nicholas of Flüe (Nicholas "of the cliff-face"), an interesting personality of the Middle Ages who was able to mediate successfully between warring parties and who used to rest his head on a stone as a pillow at night.

Occasionally when mentioning an artwork, or exhibition, that did not belong to the local brand, it would be greeted by silence, as if it were bad manners to bring up a reminder of a world outside. This phenomenon did not seem to refer to a single art field, and one did not have to talk about painting to be confronted with this as a prevailing view. Over time, I learned to smile and nod when my offer of an observation from the outside was parried with the counter recommendation – one should not look outward, but inward – or at least to the local art scene. Which is undoubtedly useful as a tool in a self-awareness seminar but not in art education. Art is about curiosity, expression and dialogue, not just obsession with the private.

Students who were mainly engaged in two-dimensional work – drawing, printmaking, painting – often fell readily under the spell of ISI. Many lost themselves in the production of meditative, indisputably beautiful but completely untouchable works. The making of a canvas, for example, was elevated to such a pure act of sacred ritual that one became wary of touching it, let alone to brazenly slap paint on it. Even the brushes seemed so infinitely more attractive when arranged in neat bunches or hung in rows on the studio wall instead of lying dirty, encrusted with paint and criss-crossed on the floor. A brush and its pictorial potential was already treated like a work of art and not as a tool with which to make one.

The studios were often tidy, and as frozen in their orderliness as showcases in which unmade but potentially tremendously beautiful works floated under glass. Of course, with such a fetishism, painting must turn into something resembling a sheet of coloured glass, a colour test, a compression of material, or a piece of cloth laid in mathematically determined folds upon the floor, and at all costs it must subjugate, eradicate if possible, the boorishly adolescent figuration that is bound quite unceremoniously to gatecrash and piss on the parade.

Painting crap

Unfortunately, the creative process is not a sterile laboratory for counting the bristles of your paintbrush but a messy, contradictory and risky affair that knocks you on your arse not just once but multiple times – not just as a student but throughout your painting career. It usually takes many mistakes and failures for something really good to come out in the end and, more often than not, it's those very mistakes and failures that end up making the work interesting. Having time to experiment through trial and error, time to practice, to fall on your arse and pick yourself up again for the next round, is what years of study are there for.

But if the concept of ISI could be radiated into a student's DNA early enough, she could be readily steered from great calamity and the squirming embarrassment of making a figurative faux pas onto a narrow-gauge track where though there are pleasantries to discover, everything is germ-free and under guarantee.

If the sacredness of ISI was additionally combined with the Helvetic art framework of strict concept, figurative painting often seemed to find itself in the role of a secret lover with whom many wished to have an affair but didn't dare to – retired teachers of ISI included, who occasionally confided their wistful regrets in my ears. I was much more concerned, however, by the many students who revealed their reluctance to do *this kind of work* in the school's studios, finding it safer to paint privately at home so as not to jeopardise their good BA grades – they'd seen what disaster could descend from on high should they do *it* openly, and should *it* then be put on trial in front of a perennially inimical jury.

That coy secrecy of the figurative was also relayed in the experience of another figurative painter in Zurich who recounted to a group of students on a studio visit that it had been impossible to paint in her art school, and that she had only dared begin some years after leaving the stricture of her educational years behind her. Ditto with another artist in St. Gallen, to whom figurative painting in her school training had been expressly forbidden. Or another colleague who confided that as soon as you've got a figure in your painting you've got a flippin' big problem – and he didn't mean in negotiating it with the paint but with the art audience. The more I spoke to artists about their experiences, the more these regretted and regretful "dittos" recurred.

But ... if you want to learn about painting, you have to go through a phase of painting crap. Then, sooner or later, the naive conception of picture-making and the surge of emotion are over, the technical knowledge, the craft component is learned, and the actual painting is well under way.

This embarrassing phase is practically unavoidable for both art students who dedicate themselves to painting and for old hands too: you grope in one paint pot after another, in private and with guidance in the student phase, until you have discovered your personal balance between material, format, motif, etc. Figuration appears, dissolves again; for some it remains as a required component, for others it disappears completely – and suddenly is back again.

What I had hitherto regarded as a stink-normal phase in a student painter's development was here considered treacherous, even a danger to the reputation of the art department. There was a long phase when students planning their BA exhibition in figurative painting were sometimes warned off, as such final projects could disgrace and make ridiculous not just the student but the school. At that time jury members invariably had little knowledge and experience of the discipline. To them, figurative painting was done and dusted and had been thrown off a cliff many decades before. They had lost the ability to approach it and often didn't know how to ascertain and evaluate its qualities. I too found these juries intimidating at first, feeling like I was peddling some illicit substance with potentially dire consequences, with some students of painting barely scraping through.

At least the art school was open enough to keep on employing me; I recently learned through a museum curator that a nearby cantonal art school had cleared out all its figurative painting tutors in 2011, apparently because they considered *it* irrelevant for the school's curriculum. In another art school, the designated sculpture lecturer began teaching painting because though the students were clamouring for it, no designated painter-teacher was on the staff.

Of course, wherever in the world one participates in art education there is always someone in authority trying to control the direction and mode of development. Partialities within art schools normally mirror those of the wider art community so the curriculum is inevitably influenced by the prevailing cultural elements of the time and place. Designing a course of study inherently involves prescribing ground rules and *modi operandi* – which are well meant and intended to lead the students to a good result. But all doctrines, however inviolable, can wear thin over time so they need to be regularly reassessed and overhauled. It is very often the students who recognise when something has become formulaic or outdated and who then begin to agitate for what they need, instigating change for themselves because they want to say something different and authentic.

Recently I was chatting on the phone with a good friend from the UK who had studied art in the 1950s and later taught. He recalled that at the time, the annual "Young Contemporaries" exhibition always featured the same selection of styles: submissions from art students at the Slade School of Art looked like work by David Bomberg;[46] those from the Royal College all looked like Pop Art; and those from Leeds and Newcastle tended towards a very narrow abstraction arising from a new programme of study instigated by Victor Pasmore and Harry Thubron called "Basic Design".[47]

Basic Design was the first attempt to introduce a formalised art education that consciously refused a romanticist and intuitive approach to art. The new way of teaching was unsurprisingly derived from the Bauhaus and, yes, was mainly based on the teachings of the Swiss artist Johannes Itten, with whom we are already familiar. Basic Design offered a systematic method of training students in understanding the qualities of line, pattern, shape and colour and their interactions, freed from object or figure. The tasks given "ranged from exercises in drawing in a relatively free manner to others calling for order and precision, with exercises acting simply as a starting point from which students could develop their work and ideas".[48] Colour theory was then the holy grail of foundation teaching and its holy book, Itten's colossus publication, *The Art of Colour*, was to be found in every art school library.

My friend was interested in the new approach but was at the same time suspicious that Basic Design was pushing the students towards a very narrow abstraction. He enrolled incognito as a student for a summer course in Norfolk led by Harry Thubron and Norbert Lynton.[49] "Interestingly all the Basic Design courses at that time were not at Art Schools but University Art courses," which added intellectual and academic weight.[50] It was said of Thubron that he was immensely charismatic, and indeed the course in the wonderful setting of Boxford was a pleasure. "But on every project it was easy to predict at the outset what would get approval or not and students acted accordingly so that the look of the work across the student body appeared very similar. The quality of the outcome was certainly shifted up a notch or two but it had lost the authenticity of trial and error. It was a quick way up the scales but without personal identity ... The Basic Design courses were, in essence, to be primarily an essential visual language applicable to all the visual arts, which was admirable but flawed and eventually became fairly formulaic, particularly in Fine Art. It was a means of upgrading to twentieth-century modernism and, in particular, abstraction as the instigators like Pasmore and Thubron were themselves abstract painters."[51]

Basic Design was not without controversy in its day, and even today the merits and blind spots of the method are debated. While Pasmore was teaching at King's College, Newcastle-upon-Tyne, until the early sixties, he developed such an animosity towards the life room that he would have shut it down had other departments not been using it, but later his close colleague and ally, Richard Hamilton, went back to teaching exercises based on figuration, though by then Pasmore himself had gone into retirement.

So it transpires that both Britain's and Switzerland's art schools have been similarly influenced, though perhaps to different degrees. The question of whether we are teaching hand or heart is central to the tussle between the rational, anti-sensorial approach and that of the romantic-intuitive. In British art education, a hybrid compromise seems to have been agreed upon. I often wonder what such a compromise would look like in Switzerland and think immediately of the rich, discursive, if quarrelsome friendship between the writers Max *the Rational* Frisch and Friedrich *the Romantic* Dürrenmatt before they unfriended one another.[52]

Don't try, DO IT

One of the best pieces of advice I ever received in my art education was something so prosaic, so utterly mundane as to be classified in the column of generally applicable, everyday-life advice covering every form of procrastination: *Don't try, DO it!* Yes, I know, that sounds more like a slogan for a DIY builders' merchant, but it nevertheless became one of my own mantras, not only in the studio, where loafing around only attracts the *black dog* of depression, but with nearly all art-related processes.

Trying is pussyfooting around on the sidelines in the vain hope that someone else will come along and do it for you – or hold your hand while you put your toe in the water. "Doing" is direct, immersive, self-responsible and committed engagement with the core of something – not always a satisfying process – in the certainty that this is the *only* way something can materialise. "Doing" is a testament to the sheer tenacity and dogged determination necessary to exist as an artist and to make one's own way, both in the studio and in the wider world into which one takes one's work and makes it visible to others. As much as painting enriches, it is not all just "Joy shall be yours in the morning!"[53]

The concept for the painting module at the university in Central Switzerland developed together with two colleagues was therefore quite simple: if you want to learn to paint and explore picture making, you have to paint, not build pristine stretcher frames and spend months on preparing the canvas or grind pigments with pestle and mortar or pluck out the hairs of a pine marten's tail to make your brush. All that has its place and is very interesting, but it doesn't necessarily help when it comes to rolling up your sleeves and getting to the dirty work of applying paint in a way that allows imagery to emerge.

So we abandoned canvas and other respectable supports, hauled in rolls of cardboard and the cheapest paints in large quantities and herded the students over a few *parcours* painting exercises that left them no time for long intellectualising or self-doubt. Once unzipped from their painter's block, they plunged into their own painting adventures, let it rip – and had fun.

Only in a second phase was analysis and reflection of the work in plenum important – but then clearly, because it highlighted that the experience of *doing* is key and that in "mistake-making" lay the greatest development potential. You first need to suspend disbelief and switch off your own permanent self-criticism, in order to allow the sort of blundering *trial and error process* on which knowledge is based. You can't do it in your head or by proxy – so you may as well jump with both feet into the quagmire.

The fact that everyone was exposed to the same process of finding answers to painting problems with and through painting, and not switching to another medium or approach, made the painting module real, substantial and successful for everyone. Besides, it was contagious. And it was actually painting.

Verbal feedback from former students, whom I sometimes met at exhibitions years later, indicated that for them, in addition to the expansion of practice, it was above all speaking about painting in tutorials both during and after working sessions that had been decisive – in particular, the possibility of naming exactly what was looking interesting and why, where a painting was too stiff and lacked tension and what the next intervention could be to solve a visual problem.

This is also the internalised dialogue that the painter gets into the habit of with her works: she does not create perfect works in genius mode, but develops paintings around mistakes and failures.

Now the painterly conversation as a crucial part of the painting process had obviously not been cultivated in the art department of this school for a long time, because none of the permanent lecturers had seen themselves as painters and the conversation about painting had either been lost or never learned. In spite of the wonderful "Raum für Farbe", a magnificent colour and pigment palace with binders, crystallised varnish – all the raw materials for the production of paintings with drawer upon drawer of pull-out colour-test plates showing how pigments react with certain binders, the bridge to the squelchy world of paint on canvas was still missing a few rungs. A language for painting needed to be reinstated as seriously as representational painting itself.

I think we were successful. The six-week module would kick-start something every year, which I continued to care for throughout the semester in individual discussions and other painting inputs. The module, which was originally limited to three years, became a fixed feature of the school and still runs today. But, more importantly, a whole new generation of figurative painters emerged not just from the "fine art" side but from design and illustration as well, unimpressed by the still-standing verdict that their discipline is not an art form but a recreational *pastime*. They don't care. They just paint.

From the horse's mouth

One reason for the success of this annual six-week painting module was the fact that two of the lecturers were not teachers in their main profession but artists with painting as their core discipline, who therefore drew from their practice and showed little patience with theory bubbles: painting is done, not thought. Or in other words, it's a way of life that has been committed to uninterruptedly since prehistoric times; it therefore represents a huge cultural heritage and still touches the roots of the human condition.

Teaching painting is not teaching the rules of visual etiquette by rote but draws from the same well of creativity that feeds painting itself. One curtails not only oneself but also the present if one dwells continually on a eulogy for the death of painting in the modern age – Painting shrugs its shoulders and simply lives on, unimpressed, alive and kicking, even in central Switzerland. The second reason for success with the module was attributable to our colleague, who, as an art historian *in love* with painting, could convey its qualities in a robust language, drawing also on Wölfflin's terminology in a frank, personal and accessible manner.

Nevertheless, our module did not solve the recurring difficulties of getting students who were painters successfully through the BA jury process year after year. On a number of occasions I had to personally assure the department that I would take responsibility for the successful completion of a student's degree show. Only then was the student allowed to continue in the medium of choice.

I also learned the hard way that a tactical approach to the presentation of work was essential. That meant, for example, working with large immersive formats that together form an installation. Or building A-frame supports so that the paintings shown on them become objects. Or detaching the canvases from the stretcher frame and letting them hang overlapping one another. Or drawing a mind map or grid on the wall as an extended visual and contextual frame that holds the smaller works together. Or, in other words, all the diversionary tactics that allow painting to crack the art code and be perceived as something that is not just painting. *Well, whatever it takes ...*

By the time I was starting to think about moving on from the art school, we had had some great successes.

So can figurative painting permanently take its place side by side with the other respectable art forms *en Suisse*? Or is its reappearance merely a flash in the pan? Will it be accepted again, seen anew, recognised by the gatekeepers of the art establishment who bear the responsibility for showing and conveying art? What does it take for figurative painting to stay on course?

It would seem that all the essential ingredients have come together for figurative painting to successfully muscle in and hold its own. For the younger generation have not only discovered it as a more or less unoccupied niche and, supported by lecturers like me, taken up their brushes again, some will also become – or already are – the curators and critics of tomorrow, with an eye that can actually *see* figurative painting and find no conflict between it and other art forms. They bring back an old skill set anew, one that can see representational painting, evaluate it and ultimately mediate it to others. These younger-generation artists and art commentators are already handing on this new skill set to others. They're not afraid of it, do not feel the need to barricade the castle and pull up the drawbridge as soon as a few fleshy paintings rock up. The figurative *and painterly* in painting coexist easily with everything else.

And so here we can witness the great and roving art beast in action, picking up on half-remembered scents, gathering up swirling eddies at the fringes of its body and dragging them into the main current.

The curious case of the painter-lecturer

One of the oddities of working as an artist-teacher in Central Switzerland was the shyness of the art department to acknowledge the exhibiting success of the painter. The more prestigious the show, the less likely it would be noticed. This progressed to such a ridiculous extent that I once was asked, in a convivial round with four perplexed museum curators, where everyone was and why the art department didn't make a coach excursion with the students, as they had done for other colleagues' shows.

These weren't piddling exhibitions but big solo shows in respectable museums with sponsorship from Pro Helvetia, my first real successes in Switzerland. God knows such events are hardly an everyday occurrence and other art schools contacted me to request guided tours with an artist talk for their students ... I could only shrug wordlessly in response – I mean, what can you say?

Was this the quiet, assimilation of new material from outside without an acknowledgement of cause and effect? I once overheard a fine fellow announce to a group of students that it was fine to rip my work off, as I had no role to speak of in the art world, so perhaps my success as an artist was perceived as a betrayal of my role as socially cohesive teacher: a round of applause for the nurturing woman! – but the successful painter?

Well, it certainly seemed that even though the department had begun to rejoice in the success of the generation of new young painters now entering the art world, there was a reluctance to give much of a nod to the imported artist-teacher accompanying them. Perhaps they considered it a phenomenon akin to spontaneous combustion rather than being brought out over long years of work and interaction with the students. It's a miracle! Figurative painters popping up out of nowhere like mushrooms after the rain – it must be the good Swiss air!

Of course, an art school is first and foremost a platform for the students to get what they require in order to move forward and embark on their own careers as artists. Role models, though, undeniably play a part here – which is why art schools actively seek capable teachers who are also thriving as artists. They not only fruitfully impart know-how to the students in class but are also standard bearers of the possible future careers that the students in the BA have in mind. Effectively, this is the trajectory that the art course is "advertising" when it attempts to recruit students each year. What does it say about the students' future career prospects if only a few teachers also have fruitful art careers? So if lecturers can show their work in solo exhibitions at well-known museums, that would seem to be something for the school to celebrate and show to its students to demonstrate that success is possible. More than that, if it is female lecturers who are succeeding as artists in a still undeniably male-dominated *industry*, and two-thirds of the students in the art department are female, would it not be ... appropriate, beneficial, even inspiring to visit these exhibitions?

The art school campus had by then moved to a new site in an industrial area outside of the city and the department had implemented curriculum changes that I didn't much like, partly in response to funding cuts caused by the canton's lowering of corporation tax. I began to feel less and less at ease in my role as art lecturer and constantly disturbed in my practice as an artist not least because the paperwork required became so overblown.

But most of all, I became tired of the perpetual attempts to transform the successful yearly painting module by turning it into an interdisciplinary course. Bonkers.

It was time to go, so I handed in my notice. The school had been a home to me, and I had been happy to work for it, but I didn't want to become a grouchy lecturer who, by 3 p.m. was already thinking of nothing but a warm bath, a Rioja and an evening with the eReader in order to continue to have lecturer status and a good salary.

At the request of the management, I postponed my departure until the art department had settled into the new curriculum and the new building, because they had not yet found another painter who also had competence and experience as a lecturer.

On finally leaving the following year, I received a standard letter from the administration as a farewell party, asking me, Frau Lumsden, to hand over my badge and keys and to check whether all emails on my @school.ch address had been deleted, because they were taking it – and me – offline at the end of the month. That was it with the farewell. Heartfelt and silent.

It had made me proud to rise from a temping tutor without a contract to a tenured BA-level lecturer. It still makes me proud that after my dozen years of teaching, figurative painting had regained a foothold and that a new generation of painters could emerge. The department hired new painting teachers to carry on the work. My part was done.

The Foreign Police in St. Gallen had long since forgotten me, and anyway I was now a Swiss citizen – though still not eligible to enter the hallowed halls of *Innerschweizer Inn* ... ah, fuck it.

Well, my lecturing days are behind me now. Sorry, Helene, I broke my promise never to teach again, probably under the influence of that old Plantagenet crook Richard the Third who, still a metre and a half under the car park tarmac, crossed his finger bones and made it all a lie.

I can now reinstate the promise *never* to teach again, again. (Well, maybe just a few days a year ...?)

40 The magical parallel world of Narnia is the main setting of the seven children's novels *The Chronicles of Narnia* by C. S. Lewis (1989–1963).

41 The Red Square lectures were initiated by Cheryl Kaplan and Mark Reynolds, who produced four contemporary art forums in 1995/96. The format was continued for a further four forums at the Royal Academy of Arts by Gerwyn Havard, Rachel Lumsden and Julie Neat in 1997.

42 Norman Rosenthal was Secretary of Exhibitions for the Royal Academy of Art, 1978–2008.

43 In recent times there have been two large fires in the Royal Academy – in 1997 and 2006.

44 HRT = Hormone Replacement Therapy

45 *Bild* is the German word for "pictures". *Bildli* is the diminutive, so essentially means "little pictures"; Migros is the largest Swiss supermarket and the Klubschule is a group of adult education programmes initiated by the brand of the Swiss Migros group providing courses throughout Switzerland including art hobby courses.

46 David Bomberg (1890–1957) was an influential British painter whose works explored the zone between figuration and abstraction.

47 Victor Pasmore (1908–1998) was a pioneer of abstract art in Great Britain; Harry Thubron (1915–1985) was a

British artist, art theorist and art teacher who introduced Basic Design courses in Leeds.

48 Elena Crippa and Beth Williamson, “Basic Design”, in id. (eds.), *Basic Design,* exh. cat., London: Tate Britain, 2013, p. 8.

49 Norbert Lynton (1927–2007) was a British art historian and art critic.

50 Interview by Rachel Lumsden with David Willetts, artist and former head of the Fine Art Department at Nottingham Trent University.

51 Ibid.

52 Max Rudolf Frisch (1911–1991) was a Swiss playwright and novelist; Friedrich Dürrenmatt (1921–1990) was a Swiss author, dramatist and a proponent of epic theatre.

53 Quote of a line of the song “Carol of the Field Mice”, from the children’s book by Kenneth Grahame (1859–1932), *Wind in the Willows,* London: Methuen, 1932.

10

Covid asks the question – "Art, what's it for?"

Anyway, here we all are, two years into Covid's *New Normal*. In the feature pages, art discourse has gone a little bit mushy and shapeless, like an over-washed sock.

But hang on ... important developments are coming in on the art scene as we speak. The title in the *NZZ*'s culture section from 19 May 2020 flashes: "As unreasonable as youth – we all believe in the great fairy tale of contemporary art as investment object. Yet the dynamics of the global art business thrive precisely on its irrational frenzy."[54] Wow! Alert the media! *NZZ* art critic Philipp Meier's got a gun and he's not afraid to shoot.

I put my coffee cup down, spread the paper flat on the kitchen table and read on. Due to Covid and the grinding halt the art world has had to endure under Covid restrictions, the colossal blind spot of the art market has become quite clearly visible, says Mr Meier. A whole industry profits from the fact that contemporary art, often fresh from the studio, is shifted back and forth around the globe for ever-increasing amounts of money. The market logic is simple:

what is expensive *must* be good. The high prices alone are a seal of quality.[55]

Brace yourself and hang onto your knickers, chaps, the emperor's clothes are coming off! Mr Meier valiantly shines his torch onto naked and pale skin and the sight is not pretty: the art market is not about art after all but about ... money. Awesome! Totally dig what you're saying, Phil. An earth-shattering revelation, which clearly without a global pandemic, could never have come to light.

Except remember the Beckhams, who in 2012 bought a baby monitor embellished by Damian Hirst, which although declared artistically worthless, was immediately valued at 10,000 pounds sterling and more, thanks to Hirst's position in the art world? A story with eye-dabbing value: while still in the cot, little Harper Beckham got a Damian Hirst all of her very own.[56] The phenomenon of one big brand name buying another big brand name dominated art news for weeks on end, and without anyone getting excited about it – drove up the value of the plastic gadget even further. The monitor will doubtless be coming to Christies for auction in due course unless ...

Is Mr Meier the man to finally and unequivocally name and shame this *courant normal*? Will he be the one to bring people back to the artwork with different eyes ... instead of bidding for Non-Fungible Tokens and feeding on resale value? My hopes fly high – because almost anything can happen in Covid times.

But no. Delirium and normal service resume in due course as I reach the closing paragraph of the article. There, intrepid journalist Meier, perhaps remembering his own Faustian bargain, veers suddenly away from his critical trajectory and lands a truly surprising twist:

> "Because art itself refuses the principle of utility, whoever buys art participates in it in a completely different way: he shares with it a subversive act of revolt .... This complicity frees us a little from all utilitarian constraints. Yes, it even gives back the

art lover something of the great freedom of youth: for when were we last so unreasonable as in our wilder days of adolescence?"[57]

And so the very core and essence of art passion is ... nostalgia. The irrational (eye-wateringly expensive) art purchase is declared as a hot wire right into the golden fountain of eternal youth – at least for the buyer (ah, now we know why billionaires with their radical life extension plans are so keen to spaff cash on art as well as inject billions in gerontological research). For the gallerist the half million bucks and a normal life span is likely to be enough.

My coffee suddenly seems to taste a bit like soapy dishwater. Meier has not just pontificated over art and its purpose – but declared the art market as holy.

That's something like what Alfred Hitchcock coined as the "ice-box scene" or fridge logic: the huge hole in the plot that only occurs to you later, back home from the movies, as you're pulling a chicken wing from the fridge – or upon reading Mr Meier's last paragraph for the fourth or fifth time.

Wouldn't there have been something else to say about what art is for?

When I encounter good art, the stream of the unformed and wordless in me is given form and expression for a precious moment and connects me with the complexity, the ambivalences, the constant shape-shifting of the world. This moment reconciles my inner life with the outer and allows me to travel back and forth between them. This multidimensional journey is only possible because the artist has done it before and paved the way for it with her work.

Artists have always done this for the collective, whether as cave paintings, carvings of a medieval chapter house, woodblock prints by Kuniyoshi or installations by Cornelia Parker. That is why art has always nurtured and challenged and pushed us to connect, to understand and to change. That is both its power and its legitimacy.

So what are the alternatives to the price equals quality issue? How will the post-Covid art market work? How will it relate to its pre-Covid rituals? Will the art fairs with their huge ecological footprint – because of the many energy-intensive transports – still exist? Will Art Basel be throwing away the carpets again after one week's use or will it recycle, upcycle and reuse like the Biennale in Venice? What should be left behind, what could have been reimagined?

Perhaps you could pick up on that another time, Mr Meier, instead of sneaking off with a tepid – *Just kidding guys, carry on, carry on!*

And I do indeed carry on, Mr Meier, painting in the studio.

In the meantime, I have been bolstered by the splendid news that William Shatner, alias *Captain Kirk*, has become Jeff Bezos's new space mascot, soon to be launched to celestial heights in a rocket that appears to be a gigantic dildo. Also, the mathematical formula for happiness has been discovered[58] – I'm sure we all breathed a collective sigh of relief at these great tidings.

It seems that happiness is mainly based on lowering one's expectations, not so completely that one immediately falls into a permanent depression, but enough to be pleasantly surprised when things work out better than expected. I think this is very good advice, not only with regard to the mental blossoms of art critics, but also with regard to painting in the studio during Covid time.

54 Philipp Meier, "So unvernünftig wie die Jugend" (As unreasonable as adolescence), in *Neue Zürcher Zeitung*, 19 May 2020, p. 27.

55 Ibid. Orginal quote in German: "Jetzt aber sehen wir den blinden Fleck des Kunstbetriebs ganz deutlich. Und das ist nicht unbedingt beruhigend. Denn erkennen wir plötzlich die wahren Beweggründe unserer Passion für die Kunst, kann es gut sein, dass der globale Kunstmarkt von heute auf morgen implodiert. Wie eine Fata Morgana könnte er sich vor unseren Augen in nichts auflösen: dieses Phänomen, dessen Mechanismen niemand je wirklich plausibel zu erklären vermochte ... genauer hinschauen wollte doch gar niemand. Wieso auch? Eine

ganze Industrie lebte gut vom Kunstbetrieb. Angefangen bei den Kunstschaffenden und weiterführend über Galeristen und Kuratoren, Messeorganisatoren und Kunstkritiker, Auktionatoren und Restauratoren, Transportunternehmer und Versicherer profitierte man davon, dass neue, junge, oft atelierfrische Gegenwartskunst rund um den Globus für immer höhere Geldbeträge hin und her geschoben wurde. So gab es keinen wirklichen Grund, zu fragen, warum das alles so ist, wie es ist, nämlich: In materieller Hinsicht ist Kunst oft von geringem Wert, und für rein geistige Inhalte Unsummen zu bezahlen, wenn man ihrer auch in Museen, Ausstellungen und Kunstbänden teilhaftig werden kann, leuchtet eigentlich nicht ein."

In English translation: "Now we clearly see the blind spot of the art industry. And that is not altogether reassuring. For if we suddenly realise the true motives behind our passion for art, it may well be that the global art market implodes overnight. Like a mirage, it could dissolve into nothing before our eyes: this phenomenon whose mechanisms no one has ever really been able to plausibly explain ... no one even wanted to take a closer look. Why should they? An entire industry made a good living from the art market. Starting with the artists and continuing to gallery owners and curators, fair organisers and art critics, auctioneers and restorers, transport companies and insurers, they profited from the fact that new, young contemporary art, often fresh from their studios, was shifted back and forth around the globe for ever-increasing amounts of money. So there was no real reason to ask why everything is the way it is: in material terms, art is often of little value, and paying vast sums for purely intellectual content when one can also partake of it in museums, exhibitions and art books doesn't really make any sense at all."

56 Marina Hyde, "The Beckhams give little Harper her very own Damien Hirst", in *The Guardian,* 19 April 2012.

57 Meier, "So unvernünftig wie die Jugend" (see n. 54). Original quote in German: "Und weil sich Kunst selber dem Nützlichkeitsprinzip verweigert, hat, wer Kunst kauft, noch auf eine ganz andere Weise Teil an ihr: Er teilt mit ihr einen subversiven Akt der Revolte. Darin aber besteht ein Gutteil der Passion für die Kunst: Diese Komplizenschaft befreit uns ein Stück weit von allen utilitaristischen Zwängen. Ja, sie gibt dem Kunstliebhaber gar etwas von der grossen Freiheit der Jugend zurück: Denn

wann waren wir letztmals so unvernünftig wie in unseren wilderen Tagen der Adoleszenz?”

58 Equation for happiness: $(t)=w_0+w_1\Sigma j=1t\gamma t-jCRj+w_2\Sigma j=1t\gamma t-jEVj+w_3\Sigma j=1t\gamma t-jRPEj$. Established at University College London in May 2021.

11

Painting!

The beginning of a painting comes from the desire to ask: What happens if ...? The answer only becomes visible when you give yourself a kick and set down a mark of paint on the canvas, which, in response, demands a second blob of paint. This is a kind of loop, in which one mark leads to another, allowing a visual dialogue to develop, sometimes without map or compass. Where one painting ends, a next one begins in response to all the questions raised by the painting before it. This is the urgency of painting.

"Urgency" has become a buzzword for painting. Curator Hans-Ulrich Obrist calls painting an "urgent medium today", referring to this urgency – as if it were an entirely new phenomenon.[59] That's not true, of course. Urgency – perhaps even desperate desire – has always been the defining force of painting. Painters have known this for a long time. That is also the reason why painting never pops its clogs, even if it has been declared dead from many sides.

Matter and representation – the quantum-physical fold

Malerei, Malen, Gemälde: Painting as genre, painting as action and painting as a work of art – these three nouns in German are all united in the single English term "painting". The root noun "paint", on the other hand, can only be translated into German as "die Farbe", and this single word stands both for "colour", as in a rainbow of, and "paint", the physical, colour-carrying substance as matter; the material that stains, runs, sticks, smells, smears.

Painting is therefore always also the presence of the material substance, with its own physical and chemical properties and idiosyncrasies. Paint is first and foremost matter that is applied to other matter – to the picture support, where the greasy substance of the paint is pushed back and forth during the painting process.

If a blob of paint is applied in a way as to be recognised as, say, a "ship" by the viewer, then the paint matter is being additionally used to depict – or represent – an object, without losing its original character as *the stuff of paint*. This is painting as representation – or figuration. For me, the real core of painting lies in this quantum-physical fold between matter and representation, there, where a white splodge is simultaneously both a paint clod of titanium white and a stealth warship. Wave-particle duality, a basic principle of quantum mechanics, tells us that at any one time a particle is simultaneously both particle (matter) and wave (light). Einstein once commented on the problem of these "two contradictory pictures of reality; separately neither of them fully explains the phenomena of light, but together they do."[60] It's the same with painterly figuration, which displays the simultaneous duality of material (the stuff of paint) and the representation of a figurative motif. Depending on how you look at them and from what distance, all the marks of the painting can therefore be read as both abstraction *and* figuration.

Or, in other words, painting is the sexy form of quantum physics. Sexy because it is such a palpable experience with and through the senses.

Good figurative painting doesn't lose visual tension if the viewer looks at it first from a distance and then from very close – in fact, the way a painting changes with relative distance is decisive for its quality and crucial to visual suspense. Viewed from further away, one focuses on what is depicted; the entire painting as a whole coalesces into a representational image; but on moving closer, one's gaze switches to abstract perception of the dabs, flecks, clods and pools of the paint matter close-up, while the illusion of what is depicted fades. Painting between representation and paint matter is in motion all the time and changes its state because it oscillates between the one and the other.

It can be compared to the moment when a wave breaks on the beach: one minute it's a tightly compact and forward-moving ridge of oscillatory particles, but when the amplitude reaches a certain point and the crest overturns, it is a flat fan of spray and foam.

Implicitly the painting process is always a negotiation between the paint matter and the intended representation. Paint refuses gestures of domination and becomes dead and flat when one tries to force it or subjugate it, it's not a servant but its own mistress.

Bending the grammar of paint without breaking it, pushing the representational motif almost to the point of dissolving – where the realm of paint as matter begins, but doing that without betraying the figurative elements or losing them completely – these are the key elements allowing the painting to remain true to itself and its parameters. For it is central to good painting that a work corresponds to itself and its own set of rules. For each work has its own variables and determines its own parameters. If one respects this and can enjoy this fundamental characteristic, then one is already on the way towards good painting.

Craft

Craft is a part of painting, but this doesn't mean doggedly following the rules of the "old masters". Craft means knowing, for instance, how to make the right stretcher support, how to prepare a ground best suited to the way you want to work.

For example, in recent years I have returned to the kind of chalk ground I used to use in my twenties. Then I used it because of its brittleness and fragility when applied to non-rigid surfaces like muslin and I let it crumble on purpose – and with it the painted image. In the meantime, I have become interested in combining areas of thicker oil paint together with thin, translucent, luminous washes, sometimes in oil, sometimes in gouache – hence the return to a chalk ground, whose intense white makes the colours glow. Because I prefer the paintings to remain intact for a much longer period of time, I now use the chalk ground conventionally as intended. This means that normal stretcher frames and canvas are no longer suitable as picture supports because the brittle chalk ground is not compatible with a pliable surface. Consequently I now paint on a rigid picture support – a wooden panel.

The problem with wooden panels is the sheer weight when you want to work on large formats of 2–3 metres. Solid MDF panels of this size, for example, would be so heavy that you would need a forklift in the studio. Since I paint alternately on the wall and on the floor, I have to be able to move my formats without help, and without slipping a disc or getting a hernia.

My father served as a mechanic in the Fleet Air Arm as a very young man towards the end of the Second World War and had a good knowledge of developments in aviation. I therefore had in the back of my mind that in the history of aviation there had been constructions made of aluminium and poplar plywood, both stiff but lightweight materials. After some research I found a manufacturer in the Netherlands who offered custom-made aluminium profiles for painting panels. It was some time before I found sheets of poplar plywood at the desired dimensions that had not been treated with filler. The first prototypes had shown that defective areas repaired with filler by the producer bubbled up when the front of the panel was sized with glue and stuck with canvas. With the right "aeroplane" glue, several dozen clamps, concrete weights (which had once served as counterweights for school blackboards in a Graubünden mountain community), I discovered after a long series of tests that it is possible to adhere Dutch aluminium frames to Italian poplar plywood and cover the face with cotton duck from Bradford, England.

The chalk ground is a traditional recipe with Bolognese and Champagne chalk dissolved in rabbit-skin glue. The Champagne chalk is, counter intuitively, the cheaper of the two, slightly pink and very soft so it makes a good filling agent; the Bolognese is more costly and very white, and so it lends the ground brilliance. I apply two coats to the panels and lightly polish the surface with fine sandpaper. After one more coat of rabbit-skin glue to stop the chalk from being too absorbent, the thing is ready to roll.

Craft means understanding that the type of chassis and primer you choose for your work is already a painterly decision that will determine first the process of painting and then the outcome.

When engaged in the considerable hassle and expense of preparing the painting panels I've been using since 2017, I've often asked myself why I bother. But I know the answer. It's the sheer tactile quality of the paint on the ground, the absorbency level between it and the paint, the smoothness of the surface and the luminosity of colour that it affords, the beauty of the ground in its own right, which shimmers through between the marks of paint, making the whole canvas seem lit up from behind; but also the unexpected possibility to remove paint again more easily so that the process isn't just about putting paint on, but about taking it off again too, about drawing back into the surface and excavating down to previous paint layers.

Immersion and the continuum

Large-format paintings are immersive. I suspect that video artists who build large video installations and their curators will mock my appropriation of this adjective, but it is true: large-scale painting *is* immersive. Not only for the viewer but also and especially first and foremost for the painter herself. That it becomes immersive is to do with movement, of the eyes and of the body. Painting is a physical activity: one is constantly moving, when one steps forward to the canvas, moves away again, then back a little further. As in Laurie Anderson's song "Walking & Falling" on her album *Big Science*: "With each step, you fall forward slightly/And then catch yourself from falling/Over and over ..."

Paint is best shoved around on the canvas (or poured, or dragged, perhaps with a floor mop ...). Some works only go on the wall when I want to look at them and only when the paint has dried sufficiently to stop the paint from dribbling down, unless I want those trickle marks.

There are also times when I paint with a "dry" brush, and then I work exclusively on the wall. This is mentioned because these descriptions apply to processes of the moment – ways of working from earlier times will perhaps return again or be quite different altogether. After all, everything happens in a continuum and time has folds and pockets.

If I have painted myself into a corner and the painting looks stiff or flat or dull, often only radical measures help: I have to risk what I've already achieved – for example, by adding a pool of paint and letting it dry out for days. Drowning out elements in parts of the picture can revive a painting that has gone astray, because a new field opens up, but always with the traces and remnants of what was there before.

It may be weeks before a painting is finished but equally it may be days or even a matter of hours, made during a single session. Who knows? It all depends.

I hold the unfinished painting in the corner of my eye, at the periphery of my vision. I leave the studio and when I go back, I sneak up on it and try to catch it before it notices me – to see what it still needs or what it no longer needs.

Some images emerge slowly and are hard-won. Others come quickly – though I suspect only because the preceding work was an absolute bugger to bring about.

Almost there

With *It's almost there* – it's almost finished – a critical and treacherous phase begins shortly before completion, in which success and failure are closely entwined bedfellows, grinning at me.

There is already so much there to engage my eyes, my brain but

squint

it doesn't quite

squint

all hang together

In *Fence*, a painting where everything flows towards you, my gaze always slipped beyond the bottom edge and couldn't find its way back into the painting without effort: it was as if the painting emptied itself down there. So I painted a fence as a foreground, projecting into the picture directly from the lower edge. This redefinition of the pictorial space kept my gaze moving within the picture so it could no longer escape. The squinting stopped.

Lightning Rod – Mrs and Mr Andrews, a small homage to Gainsborough, shows a couple in front of a cloudscape and a strip of London city panorama. This work had a different problem, but with the same effect: squint.

Until I realised that the two faces in the painting trapped the gaze of the viewer. As if these were two guardian sphinxes that you couldn't escape. It had not been my intention to paint a double portrait, but of course the painting did exactly what a portrait is supposed to do: it draws the attention to the face and lets the gaze rest on its features. My painting concern, on the other hand, had been the equivalence of faces, clouds and city; I had intended to paint a panorama with people, not a portrait with cityscape as a background.

So I grabbed a broad brush and used it to draw a vertical streak of black paint from the top to the bottom of the picture, right through the face and body of the one protagonist – the lightning rod that divided the canvas into two unequal halves, allowing the view to flow freely again both to the left and right of it. The intervention could have ruined the composition and thus the painting, but can you ruin a picture that makes you squint?

In painting, one produces a series of failures that are just as important and influential as the successful paintings. However unloved and doomed to an existence in the storage cupboard they may be, without them no further development would have taken place. By the end of this pictorial journey, my interest had moved on from the figure to the landscape. Since then, with one or two exceptions, the human figure appears mostly in the distance, small, almost schematic, as an abbreviation. So the process of painting engenders change and development – you're always on the move. In many paintings a mood of uncertainty and the as yet unknown prevails; others radiate existential power. They can be industrial landscapes that sink back into an apparent idyll of nature, or depict doll-like figures that move brashly out into the world. Surprised, one stands before a thicket full of birds and finds oneself confronted with an archaic image that flickers between abstraction and figuration.

Time out of time

What does a finished painting do? It leads the eyes in loops repeatedly over its surface. This visual roving over painted terrain does what movement always does, whether walking, driving, or travelling over the surface of a canvas: internal processes are set in motion, processes in the eye when the visual rods and cones are fired up, processes between the retina and the optic nerve, processes between the optic nerve and the brain, so that thinking, memory and experience are stimulated and, right in the middle, emotion. For who can see and think without feeling at the same time?[61] In this flickering back and forth, between image, eyes, brain, psyche and back again, from within the quantum physical fold between paint matter and representation, one finds oneself neither entirely with the material substance nor entirely with the represented, neither entirely in one's own inner world nor entirely outside it, but floating in the in-between, in *time out of time*.

You remember, don't you? You were eleven, stranded in the grim reality between a family with a terminally ill father and the unbearable State Comprehensive School. Lying on the edge of the school grounds on the disused railway embankment looking at the sky, at the sycamore propellers circling down to you, slowly, hypnotically. Clearly, time is elastic and can slow down. You remember your first bike collisions and how you fly over the handlebars in slow motion and how time spreads so wide that you can think of everything at once; the tear in your jeans at the knee, the *steak and kidney pie* sitting heavily on your stomach, the pocket money you will probably forfeit because you are out later than allowed. *Time out of time:* the time outside of time. Forever in a moment.

Yes, you remember.

The inner journey with a painting begins, of course, with the painter herself: she is the first traveller with each of her works and receives that as a down payment for her endeavours. Whatever inner journey viewers make in front of a painting is a matter between it and them. To experience a painting, the viewer must allow herself to be drawn into the painting's gravitational field. The moment of looking, of engaging, is always in the present: this is why painting is always now, here in the contemporary moment, where the painting has the ability to touch the inside of the present.

And then in the spring of 2020 the present turns inside out with ... Coronavirus.

Woe Corona

In 2019 after leaving my teaching post, I laid an English garden: herringbone brick paths, brick vegetable beds with flowers in between, a rose pergola and a little white greenhouse with a decorative gable, the whole shebang. It was the best I could do for my lingering Brexit depression. To brush up on my bricklaying and cement-mixing skills, I watched *Best Brickie* on YouTube and tried not to think about whether these young brickie guys had voted to leave the EU. At the same time, I took care of a crow we had found shot and bleeding in a hazel bush and delighted in her.

The work in the studio was deliberately on the back burner: I needed a fallow period to collect myself and think about what I had done and what I wanted to do, even though there was a big exhibition at the Haus für Kunst St. Josef in Solothurn at the end of the year. I was looking forward to 2020 with optimism, anticipating new work and new inroads into the world of art.

January arrived and with it the return of my work from Solothurn. Unfortunately, a collector had balked at the size of the painting and bailed out of the sale. The van in which the gallerist drove the works back to *Suisse Oriental* broke down somewhere around Winterthur and was towed away to a godforsaken industrial park on the outskirts. I had to collect both work and the gallery owner in my own van delivering him, frozen to the bone, to the nearest station and driving the paintings back to Arbon in a melancholy mood, seriously questioning the concept of a benign universe.

In the meantime, a few new paintings are on the way in the studio; they are all a bit disparate and something of a motley crew. The one that interests me most has its roots in my photo archive, shots of tanker ships that I had taken years before in that inland port on the Yangtze. There's something about the ships, the fog and the washed-out colour into which the outlines of the urban skyline dissolve and disappear, something that draws me into painting. It's easy to push this painting to the edge of abstraction, then anchor it again on the pontoons in the foreground. I accept this image without resistance.

Then Covid strikes, sending the world into Lockdown No. 1. And with it comes the realisation that we are all embarking on a big journey into the unknown. The newspapers fill with photos of impounded cruise ships, passengers sick without permission to go ashore. And there is Wuhan with officials in Hazmat suits taking the temperature of its citizens at arm's length with white plastic thermometer guns and spraying the asphalt with disinfectant.

The Yangtze forged a connection years ago, but I only realise this now.

There are routines that can be used to kick-start the painting process, routines of small steps until you suddenly find yourself head over heels in painting. I make monoprints and little A4 works on MDF, I put the iPod on shuffle mode, fragments of audiobooks interrupt Icelandic reggae, are interrupted by Arvo Pärt or the Squirrel Nut Zippers or Fleetwood Mac ... and in this labyrinth of sounds the nasty little voice in my head that wants to teach me that all this is a waste of time anyway ... falls silent – and suddenly I'm in the middle of painting.

But Covid not only ploughs up social life but also, after a few short weeks, tampers with time. The days are long, the week is short, a lot of time on your hands but no time to do anything with it.

In the studio it feels like I am wading through molasses. The tried and tested routines to ignite the painting process ... fail. The alienation between me and painting grows and grows till I lie awake at night unable to think of anything else.

At the beginning of 2020 I had been thrilled to learn that two works of mine were to be shown in a group exhibition in a museum in Thurgau. In the meantime the exhibition is hung, but Covid has turned it into a ghost show with no one to see it. Almost overnight, everything that had given me a perspective for my work in the studio falls away, no more solo museum show in Moscow to work towards, no group show in the Museum in X, no purchase of paintings by Foundation Y, regardless that they'd already selected the work for their collection. The motor that gets me out of bed in the morning and in front of the canvas in the studio sputters and stalls.

A lonely business

Painting is a lonely business at the best of times. No one tells me what to do or whether it is worth the effort. Painting is not *performative*, I have no audience watching, cheering me on, nobody's stoking the fire. I no longer have a second job as a reason to leave the studio, no overriding structure from other work like teaching. The loss of the wider framework feels ... crippling.

I'm on the phone with two gallery owners. They are chatting about the possibility of digital representation, of virtual exhibitions that would be accessible globally via the Internet. I try to sound like this is all interesting, fine and dandy, but I'm really thinking about the curious trend with many photo apps that bleach out colours or imitate dust and scratches to dampen the high resolution of digital images. Apparently people miss the magic and melancholy of analogue photography and want to artificially recreate it.

Painting has never lost its magic, because it remains coupled to the eye and the refraction of light in its organic tissues and its fluids. It is first a sensorial medium, then a cerebral one. Painting as a representative of a "warm" way of seeing in the face of digital image worlds has recently enjoyed increased popularity.

"Yep," I reply to the gallerist on Skype, "I suppose I could do a little film of my studio and the paintings that I'm currently working on ...", but inwardly I'm stuck thinking of the big obstacle: you can't really convey painting through a digital medium. Even art professionals can suddenly be surprised by the richness, intensity and persuasiveness of the experience they get in front of an original painting after years of viewing – and rejecting – the same works online or in print.

The idea that my pictures should only be digital shadows depresses me, although I try not to be a killjoy, even if I feel like I'm running after the Pied Piper of Hamelin.

So I stand now in front of several messed-up paintings in the studio and look at them through the video lens of my smartphone. My eye gets stuck on the flatbed sander which I have started to use to sand back the failed work of the previous day, only to stand in front of the same unresolved, unredeemed images day after day with the stench of rabbit skin glue in my nostrils. I turn off the video function on my mobile phone, pull on the nitrile gloves and apply a glob of paint to one of the pictures with a rag.

"Tricky," I say a couple of days later, to the gallery owner, when we next speak digitally. "Difficult if it's the only possible contact with the painting." A message appears on the screen, telling me that my Internet connection is unstable, and the gallerist pixelates, his voice sounding hollow and metallic. I think about the material presence of my paintings getting lost in the pixel-abyss.

One form of literacy can be replaced by another. Just as digital messaging, for example, displaces the ability to focus on longer texts such as a lengthy newspaper article or even a novel, the digital age can damage the ability to engage with, break down and read paintings. "The answer?" I wonder. "Keep looking at originals, don't settle for a copy."

Later, I leave the studio disheartened and walk out into the night away from the streetlights, past the last house in the town and into the darkness of the fields above which the Plough hangs lazily to the north-west overhead. I walk between fields of barley, take a deep breath and, looking upwards, pause in wonder: the wheels of the Plough seem to turn on their axis, no, more than that, it is as if stars were weirdly detaching from the constellation. I wonder now if the atmosphere has solar interference, whether a solar storm is hitting the Earth's stratosphere right now.

However, it is not only the wheels of the Big Dipper that roll off to the side, now a long procession of stars is also passing through towards the east, close behind each other, at regular intervals, like beads drawn by an invisible thread. Dumbfounded, gobsmacked, seized by biblical awe, I count the stars in procession. Forty at least. Satellites? Planes? No, no winking lights! Spaceships? No! No! Impossible! Military black ops? Fuck no. Angels? The last star passes through and disappears behind the ridge in the east. I stand stock-still, but my heart is thudding. Before I can find a plausible explanation, a second chain is already moving up in the west. I call my husband, he too watches the celestial events from the balcony and searches online for an answer, while I count the stars of this procession – at least seventy. They are Elon Musk's starlink Internet satellites, abhorred by astronomers. They pierce my dreams that night.

Despite my nocturnal excursion, the painting luck does not materialise in the studio the next day either and I've got the sander in my hands yet again and again I'm wearing a thicker mask than the one I go to Migros in. I don't feel great about any of these paintings that seem hardly to be there and only hold together by the skin of their teeth. I fear ... I have become an artist from the *Innerschweizer Innerlichkeit* persuasion, afraid to make a mark ... Actually, I don't feel great at all. But the misery can't be avoided. There are no tricks, no routines to avoid this failure and inertia, just as there are no tricks and no routines to remove the virus from the agenda.

Note to self

We're all familiar with the idea of artistic genius. We all have seen the one decisive moment when the artist swiftly executes a composition on a flat glass plate with fluid brushstrokes, filmed from below with a camera. Or the view from over the other artist's shoulder as he traces the flowing contours of the woman's body in brush and ink, not a pause, never a mistake. If ever there was a rod to beat the back of the artist, it's this myth of the genius at work. No wonder they never get the painting bit right in artists' biopics, I think, as I draw into wet paint with a bit of tee-shirt over my finger.

Weeks pass like this, painting stuff in, scrubbing stuff out, sanding back, occasionally reapplying gesso that has been worn so thin. I slip on paint spillage that has fled the canvas, making its way under the chassis to seep out the other side. With an aching back I realise no one can save me or do this for me. There is no way around but to plod on through. It's a daily defeat but I must pursue it like any other job.

Note to self: Apply paint to area X but be careful to leave area Y open to the white ground – at least for the time being.

Note to self: Sand that surface back again and apply a fluid layer of cobalt blue light, preferably the Norma and not the Windsor, then draw X motif into surface.

Note to self: Rinse the gouache-saturated mopheads and put them through the washing machine at 60 degrees before you start again tomorrow.

In the stunted development of Covid times I find there's a lot to be said for the sheer pragmatism of a job, and the accompanying To Do List. Better, at any rate, than constantly hitting yourself over the head with the creativity mallet. Nothing's so deflating as gearing yourself up to perform "creatively", but then I'm not a genius, of course, and never was – never could have been, because I was born a woman and have more womb than brain – or so they think.

It is eleven at night. One of the cats yowls in the courtyard. I've forgotten that I needed a wee twenty minutes ago and that I'd intended to have an early night and I'm pushing the paint around on the surface with a floor mop and a torn-up bed sheet for smearing on the oil paint. And suddenly I'm fourteen again and something simple and completely undisguised is there, something that surprises me, something that I did not plan or intend, something really embarrassing to the critical eye of the experienced painter, but nevertheless, after weeks of failure something is ... there. Naked, clumsy, limping. But alive. How difficult not to remove it immediately but instead to ... to allow it to take me by the hand and lead me deeper into painting.

It is shortly before midnight, in a sleeping village at the eastern border of Switzerland, where almost nobody knows me. So who am I now on the stroke of midnight? Am I the "lost daughter" of the London School or a Swiss artist who, with the aesthetic genes of a complete foreigner, does not belong? Am I the lecturer who fails to push the artist? The artist who suffers from no longer being a lecturer?

Well, the answer that comes is as simple and straightforward as the chimes that now echo from the nearby church tower. I am what I already was and always will be – a painter.

The tomcat is still yowling.

But tomorrow I won't be picking up the sander first thing. It will be a brush.

Or a mop.

Or a rag.

Whatever will help me put paint on and on and on.

Oh yeah.

Rachel Lumsden, 2020–2023

59 Hans-Ulrich Obrist, in *Vitamin P3: New Perspectives in Painting*, London: Phaidon, 2016.

60 "Wave-particle duality", en.wikipedia.org/wiki/Wave%E2%80%93particle_duality (accessed 6 Mar. 2023).

61 Conversation with Markus Landert, Museum Director at Kunstmuseum Thurgau Switzerland, 2017.

Acknowledgements

As the end of 2022 approaches I think with gratitude of those without whom this book would not have become a reality.

Thank you to all my friends and test-readers for their honesty, patience and constructive advice. Thanks to Charlotte Mullins (London) for her expert editing suggestions and encouragement; to David Willetts (Southwell) for multiple draft reads and for his deep and entertaining insights into the nature of art education; to Ingrid Schindler (St. Gallen) for her detailed commentary, for her love of spiciness in food and literature alike and the recommendation not to pussyfoot around. Also to Stefan Schindler (St. Gallen) for his corrections and advice. My gratitude goes to Felicity Lunn (Zurich) for her steadfast and ongoing feedback, for the accuracy with which she identified weaknesses in the text and for always pointing me in the right direction. Many thanks also to Corinne Schatz (St. Gallen), who generously shared her precise art historical knowledge and experience with me, and to Guido von Stürler (Wallenwil) for his support and candid insights into the art scene.

A big thank you to Peter Allard (London) for the many enriching conversations about painting, for his benevolent eye on early drafts, for title suggestions and for his insistence on a table of contents: Peter, you were right! Thanks to Deborah and Rob Bowman (Rotherham) for ploughing through the super clunky first draft and for spurring me on to better things. Also many thanks to Kate Martin (Nottingham) for her robust, in-depth and open-hearted feedback, for cautionary words and the onward cheer. Thanks to Bernard Jordan (Paris) and Gaby Popp Robinson

(London) for long, candid and entertaining talks about the book and the art scene. My thanks go also to Andrea Heiler (Frastanz) who looked after our flat throughout and rescued us repeatedly from piles of paper, stacks of dirty dishes and sticky tabletops.

My grateful thanks to my husband Stefan Sprenger who not only encouraged and supported me from start to finish in this writing endeavour but who eventually took on the tricky task of translating the manuscript into German.

A special place in this acknowledgement is reserved for Markus Landert, Stefanie Hoch and Cornelia Mechler of Kunstmuseum Thurgau, Kartause Ittingen: I appreciate your support very much, thank you.

Thank you to Thomas Kramer of Scheidegger & Spiess for his straightforward acceptance of the manuscript for publication, to Chris Reding at the publishing house for her competent organisation and excellent supervision of the project, and to Louise Stein, Miriam Seifert-Waibel, Simon Cowper and Maike Kleihauer who have worked on editing and correcting this essay in both languages.

Thanks too to Helen Ball (London) for her original copy editing work on earlier drafts. Katrina Wiedner (Vienna/London) I would like to thank for her special effort in creating a stunningly beautiful book design and layout.

My love and gratitude to our cherished and much-missed father, Norman Lumsden. Thank you for the ship drawings, the starry-night walks and wonderful descriptions of trees and buildings. For the tips on how to avoid shark and crocodile attacks, for your healthy scepticism towards authoritarian structures and for your willingness to shake things up, as and when required. Most importantly for your last words: Everything is about love in the end. I do believe it is, even when it's also about shaking things up.

My gratitude and affection goes also to my dear friend and collector in Switzerland, Alfred Illi (Zurich †). Thank you for your long friendship and support over many years and for all the converstaions about painting.

Nothing is a lone endeavour and without all of the above-mentioned people and institutions, the Penguins would never have got off the ice floe.

Therefore, once again, Thank you!